EARLY
CHRISTIAN
WRITINGS

EARLY
CHRISTIAN
WRITINGS

*

The Apostolic Fathers

*

Translated by
Maxwell Staniforth

DORSET PRESS
New York

This translation first published 1968.

This edition published by Dorset Press,
a division of Marboro Books Corporation,
by arrangement with Penguin Books Ltd.
1986 Dorset Press

Distributed in the United Kingdom by Bibliophile Editions

ISBN 0-88029-074-9
(Formerly ISBN 0-14-044-197-2)

The paper used in this book meets
the minimum requirements of the
American National Standard for
Permanence of Paper for Printed
Library Materials Z39.48–1948.

Printed in the United States of America
M 9 8 7 6 5

To

BETTY RADICE

critic and editor of this book
O si sic omnes

Contents

To A.L.M.

My dear Amanda,

I have not forgotten your puzzled curiosity while I was writing this book, nor the many questions you asked about 'all those old holies' and their doings. My answers at the time had to be brief; but now that the book is finished, let me try to reply a little more fully than I was able to then. As I expect you know, the first few centuries of the Church's life produced a great mass of Christian literature. A certain amount of it was apocryphal, or even heretical (which is not surprising, because when people are eagerly exploring all the implications of a brand-new religion, even the best-intentioned of them are liable to stray into bypaths that lead nowhere); but there is also a great deal that is immensely valuable, both historically and doctrinally. It is not all equally important, nor even all quite orthodox; but on the whole the Church has agreed to look on this body of literature as an authoritative embodiment of her beliefs and traditions, and as a court of appeal when theologians differ. What you will meet in this book are the earliest and most venerable examples of it: the works of a small group of men whom we know by the specific name of *The Apostolic Fathers*. In the eyes of the primitive Church the writings of these men were on virtually the same level as Holy Scripture; in fact, if things had been only just a very little different, some of them would actually have *been* Holy Scripture – and today, instead of being unknown names, as they are to nine people out of ten, they would have been familiar to every Bible reader in the world. (It would be hard to find a more striking instance of 'the little less, and what worlds away', don't you think?) Anyway, a seventeenth-century French scholar, Jean Cotelier, was the first to group these writers together in a special class by themselves, though the name, which was meant to make it clear that they were all supposed to have been personally associated with the Apostles, was the invention of a later editor, one

9

Thomas Ittig. Nowadays the group is usually understood to include Clement, Ignatius, Polycarp, Hermas, Papias, and the authors of *The Epistle to Diognetus, The Epistle of Barnabas,* and the *Didache.** The claims of the first three of these to be called Apostolic Fathers are sound enough, for almost certainly they were all disciples of some Apostle: Clement of St Peter and St Paul at Rome, and Ignatius and Polycarp of St John at Ephesus. I am afraid the other writers, whoever they may have been, have no real right to the title at all. The *Shepherd,* for example, is not really the work, as people used to think, of the Hermas who was St Paul's friend.† Nor was it the Apostle Barnabas, but probably some unknown Alexandrian, who wrote the epistle that goes by his name; and Papias, as Eusebius ‡ has pointed out, was never taught by John the Apostle, but by his namesake John the Presbyter. In the *Epistle to Diognetus,* it is true that one chapter begins, 'I was a pupil of the Apostles'; but we know now that that particular chapter is part of a quite different work, written some centuries later, so that whatever the writer meant by those words he cannot have meant them in their literal sense. As for the *Didache,* nobody has ever had any idea who wrote that; it was admitted to the select circle simply on the strength of its presumably early date and the nature of its contents. So if you want a definition of the Apostolic Fathers, all we can say is that they are certain writers who faithfully preserved the apostolic teaching and tradition between the time of the Apostles themselves and the latter years of the second century.

Nearly all their writings, as you will see, take the form of letters (the *Shepherd* and the *Didache* are exceptions). Clement, Ignatius, and Polycarp write in a manner very like that of St Paul; we find them firmly but tenderly denouncing heresies, rebuking dissensions, and exhorting to Christian morality in warmly human and affectionate missives, written simply and directly from the heart (though I cannot help thinking

* The lengthy *Shepherd* of Hermas and the *Fragments* of Papias are omitted from this book for reasons of space.

† *Romans* xvi, 14. ‡ *Hist. Ecc.* iii, 39 – Penguin edition, p. 150.

Clement's quotations from Scripture too long-winded, besides being often inaccurate). On the other hand, the *Epistle to Diognetus* and the *Epistle of Barnabas* are much less personal in character; they look like letters, but in fact they are small-scale theological treatises. Lightfoot has said that 'they resemble rather the Epistle to the Hebrews than the letters of St Paul'. All the writers in the group, however, have one thing in common: a genuine pastoral concern. They are more pre-occupied with people than with ideas. Their religion is practical, not dogmatic. The great saving truths of the Faith are pressed home again and again, but always as vital realities, urgent in their relevance to life, and not as an academic exercise. The Apostolic Fathers were not all intellectual giants, they were men of a simple and rather endearing piety, who were devoted heart and soul to a living Saviour and quite untroubled by the theological conundrums that were so soon to perplex their successors. They were fortunate enough to live and write when Christianity was still young, and something of the innocent freshness of the morning still clings to those unpretentious letters of theirs. If the ancient custom of reading them publicly in church were occasionally to be revived, they would, I think, fall pleasantly as well as edifyingly on the ears of a modern congregation. (I have seen the brethren of a religious community, when the story of Polycarp's martyrdom was read aloud to them at the midday meal, pay more attention to it than to their excellent fish pie.)

Though their writings (with the possible exception of the *Epistle to Diognetus*) have no literary merit at all, their value to posterity is inestimable. For one thing, because of the care they took to hand down intact the truths of the Gospel and the teaching of the Pauline epistles, the outburst of theological activity which followed in the next century found itself in possession of a soundly scriptural foundation. For another, they provide the student of history with the only glimmer of light, in an otherwise completely dark period, on the emerging traditions and organization of the infant Church, at a time when it was still dependent solely on its own powers and principles, and not yet on the State. But I think there are even better reasons than these why you may find them worth reading, Amanda. When you have seen the serene courage of old Polycarp, as he faces the yelling thousands in the circus with the faggots smoking and blazing about him, or the unaffected pleasure with which Ignatius looks forward to being 'ground fine by the lions' teeth to become purest bread for Christ', I hope you will come to value these nice 'old holies' for their own sakes, and will find their simple wisdom and unassuming sanctity as attractive a study as I do. That is why I have followed the advice of one of their former editors, William Reeves, who wrote as long ago as 1709 that 'it cannot but be worth while to translate some of the next best books to the Bible, so as to open a passage for the unlearned into the knowledge of the purest times of Christianity next to the Apostles, not by scraps or quotations, which are neither safe nor satisfactory, but from the entire authors themselves'.

Yours affectionately,
Max

Translator's Note

Kirsopp Lake's edition of the Apostolic Fathers in the Loeb Classical Library provides a good Greek text that is easily accessible, and so this is the one I have mainly used. But I have had no scruples in departing from it here and there in favour of an alternative reading (usually Lightfoot's) if that seemed to suit my purpose better. The translator, no less than the poet, should be allowed his occasional licences of this sort. A few notes have been unavoidable, to explain allusions or obscurities in certain passages, but I have kept these down to a minimum. If anyone needs further information, there are plenty of commentaries available. Lightfoot's great volumes of 1885/90, of course, overshadow the rest, and on most points still manage to say the last word. Newer scholarship is represented by J. A. Kleist with his annotated translations in the *Ancient Christian Writers* series (Newman Press, Westminster, Maryland, or Longmans, Green, London, 1948), and by such studies of individual fathers as Lowther Clarke's *First Epistle of Clement to the Corinthians* (S.P.C.K., London, or Macmillan Company, New York, 1937) or Virginia Corwin's excellent *St Ignatius and Christianity in Antioch* (Yale University Press, 1960). As well as the Loeb edition referred to above and a one-volume translation by Lightfoot (*The Apostolic Fathers*, 1901), there are also English, or rather American, translations by C. C. Richardson (*Library of Christian Classics*, Vol. 1; Westminster Press, Philadelphia, or S.C.M. Press, London, 1953) and E. J. Godspeed (*The Apostolic Fathers*, Harper Bros., U.S.A., or Independent Press, London, 1950). For those who are interested in the study of Essene Judaism and its possible influence on Ignatius and his contemporaries, T. H. Gaster's translation of *The Dead Sea Scriptures* (Doubleday, 1956) is a useful introduction.

*

THE FIRST EPISTLE
OF CLEMENT
TO THE CORINTHIANS

*

Clement of Rome

In the year 1628 an ancient manuscript of the Greek Bible was presented to King Charles I by the Patriarch Cyril of Jerusalem. In addition to the books of the Old and New Testaments it was also found to contain two further documents, which were described as 'the Epistles of Clement'. Until this discovery the epistles had been unknown to Western scholars, though there are frequent references to them in the works of early Christian writers. The second document proved to be in fact not an epistle but part of a sermon, and its Clementine authorship can be rejected with certainty; but in the first we now possess the earliest and most valuable surviving example of Christian literature outside the New Testament. It takes the form of a long letter addressed by the church of Rome to the sister church at Corinth, and critics are generally agreed in fixing the date of it at about A.D. 96. Since it describes the messengers entrusted with its delivery as 'men whose lives have been irreproachable from youth to age', they must have been of the second generation of Christians, which brings us up to the closing years of the first century. This explains the mention (in the opening chapter) of the Roman church's 'recent misfortunes' as a clear allusion to the notorious persecution of the Christians under the late emperor Domitian; and the most reasonable assumption therefore is that the epistle was written shortly after that persecution had been brought to an end by the assassination of Domitian in September 96.

Though the writer does not disclose his name, the unanimous opinion of the ancients attributed the composition to Clement, the contemporary bishop of Rome – known as Clemens Romanus to distinguish him from the later Clement of Alexandria. In the traditional line of bishops of the Roman church a Clement holds the third place among the successors of St Peter (the official order is Peter A.D. 62–67, Linus 67–78, Cletus 78–90, Clement 90–100), and there is no reason to deny the accepted view that in this person we have the author of the letter. But attempts to identify him any further lead only to uncertainty and disagreement. Eusebius,* on the authority of Origen, has no hesitation in affirming him to be the Clement mentioned by St Paul as one of his fellow-labourers at Philippi;† but although this is not chronologically impossible, it is in the highest degree unlikely that a member of the Philippian church and the head of the Roman community should be one and the same individual – more especially since the name Clement was a far from uncommon one at the time. Another old tradition identifies him with a certain Titus Flavius Clemens, a distinguished Roman nobleman who held the consulship in 95 and was nephew to the emperor Vespasian and a cousin of the two succeeding emperors Titus and Domitian. The belief rests mainly on a statement by the historian Dion Cassius that this Flavius Clemens was eventually executed by Domitian on the excuse of his 'atheism' (a common appellation of Christianity in the heathen world), as well as on the additional circumstance that his wife Domitilla was almost certainly a Christian herself. It is hard to believe, however, that the position of a first-century Roman consul could be compatible with the office of a Christian bishop; to say nothing of the further objection that the letter of a cultured Roman of the court circle would undoubtedly have been written in a more classical and less Jewish style than our epistle. Nevertheless, this legendary association of Clement with the imperial family may very well conceal a clue to the real state of the case. For if we accept the suggestion that the future church leader was in fact a freedman belonging to the house of Flavius Clemens, and that in accordance with custom he assumed the name of his patron at his liberation, the subsequent confusion of Clement the bishop with Clement the consul can be readily explained; and most critics are now inclined to take this view.

Towards the close of the second century a fictitious life of

* *H.E.* iii, 15 (Penguin edition, p. 124).
† *Philippians* iv, 3.

Clement was published. It can be read by the curious in the Clementine *Homilies*, and also in the *Recognitions*, though as history it is quite worthless. The truth is that we have no information about the writer except the letter itself. We can say no more than that he was deeply versed in the Old Testament scriptures – from which he quotes widely and profusely, and which have coloured his style with occasional Hebraisms – but that he knows them in the Septuagint (Greek) translation only, and betrays no actual knowledge of Hebrew. From this we may perhaps assume that he was of Greek rather than of Jewish descent. He is also familiar with the Pauline epistles to the Romans, Corinthians, and Ephesians, as well as with I Peter, James, and Hebrews; though he does not yet, of course, credit these writings with the same authority as Scripture. According to Irenaeus,* he had seen some of the Apostles and heard them preach. He is said to have met a martyr's death in about A.D. 100; though as martyrdom was conventionally ascribed to every early bishop of Rome, this is problematical.

The precise nature of his position in the Church is not clear. So far as we can tell, monarchical bishops, or sole rulers of the local congregation, were as yet unknown at Rome; indeed, Clement himself in this very letter seems to speak of bishops and presbyters as though they were identical. Moreover, there is a statement in the *Shepherd*† of his younger contemporary Hermas which says that, of two copies of a certain revelation, 'one is to be sent to Clement and the other to Grapte; and Clement shall then send it to the cities abroad, for that is his business'; and the sharing of this commission between Clement and some female servant of the Church (presumably a deaconess) does not suggest that his office at the time was one of pre-eminent dignity. It is also significant that Ignatius, writing some twenty years later to the Christians at Rome, says nothing of any episcopal ruler there, while in his other letters, addressed to Churches in his native Asia, there is invariably some allusion to their bishops. It seems therefore a plausible conjecture that

* *Haer.* iii, 3; quoted by Eusebius, *H.E.* v, 6 (Penguin edition, p. 208).
† *Vision* ii. 4.

Clement may have been one – though possibly the principal one – among several leaders of the Roman Church, and that he was especially charged with its relations with other churches; in other words, that his functions were those of a sort of foreign secretary.

The circumstances that called forth his epistle can be briefly recounted. The feuds and dissensions which had split the Corinthian church in St Paul's day had now, a generation later, sprung into new life. Some of the younger hot-heads had risen up against their lawfully appointed presbyters and thrust them out of their office. Such an action was plainly inexcusable, since the deposed ministers had at all times performed their duties irreproachably. It is probable that the quarrel was more personal than doctrinal, and occasioned by an insubordinate minority who resented the authority of their seniors. Nevertheless, though Clement expressly denounces a handful of individuals as the trouble makers, he does not hesitate to include the whole Corinthian church in his strictures; asserting that as a result of its material prosperity it had become swollen with pride, and that this had given rise to the present jealousy, strife, and disorders.

But why, it may be asked, should Rome have taken it upon herself to intervene in the domestic quarrels of the Corinthian Church? The reason lies partly, no doubt, in the keen sense of brotherhood which linked the early Christian communities together, and caused the concern of one to be felt as the concern of all. But we must also remember the special relationship which existed between these two cities. Corinth had been re-founded in 44 B.C. as a Roman colony; its government was modelled on the Roman pattern, with senators, consuls, and other magistrates, and there was a vigorous Roman element in its population. Furthermore, both Churches owned, as they believed, the same two Apostles, St Peter and St Paul, as their founders; and it was from Corinth that the latter had written his epistle to the Romans. It was therefore natural for Roman Christians to take a particular interest in the troubles of their Corinthian brethren. There is certainly no suggestion that any prescriptive authority inheres as yet in the Roman Church itself, and we do not even know whether its remonstrances in this case had any effect. All the same, it may well be that the wide influence which this epistle came to exercise in Christian circles helped to prepare the ground for the future assertion of papal claims.

At a first reading, the verdict of most people on the epistle will probably be that it is loosely put together and shows little or no continuity of thought. Clement, it must be admitted, is not a clear or orderly thinker. He is diffuse and rambling, and it is not always easy to see what the different sections of his discourse have to do with one another. But a more attentive reading will cause the earlier judgement to be revised. It will then be noticed that from all the apparent inconsequence and irrelevance there emerges a single ever-present idea. The fact is that from beginning to end of the letter Clement is deeply preoccupied with the heinous sin of pride: the pride and jealousy of a few ambitious malcontents which has split the church of Corinth and destroyed its peace. Consciousness of this evil urges him to combat it with vehemence, and to bring every possible weapon to bear upon it; and the result is the rather confused jumble of warnings, arguments, appeals, and exhortations which stream from his pen without order or system, and range over a wide and varied field. At one moment he may be ransacking the scriptures for examples of pride punished and humility rewarded; at the next, launching into an eloquent eulogy of the workings of the physical universe, as an object lesson in harmonious cooperation; or again, taking a survey of the military world, with its graded ranks and duties, in order to demonstrate the necessity of obedience to lawful authority and the mutual interdependence of different elements in a community. So the reader may find it helpful to carry in his mind for reference, as he turns the pages, certain basic concepts, such as Repentance, Humility, Self-abnegation, Obedience, Love, Unity, which will serve as signposts to keep him from losing his way through the epistle; and if at times the precise purport or relevance of a particular passage eludes him, he may be sure that its intention is to bring about one or other of these desirable states. For as Clement himself says in another context, 'there are many gates that stand open'; and it is by throwing open as many different gates as he can, that the bishop hopes to induce the erring sheep of Corinth to repent of their pride, learn the grace of humility and find their way back to fraternal peace and unity within the Christian brotherhood.

The *First Epistle of Clement* was widely known and held in very great esteem by the early Church. It was publicly read in numerous churches, and regarded as being almost on a level with the inspired scriptures. (One document, the sixth-century *Apostolical Canons*, actually includes it among the books of the New Testament; but there are reasons for believing the entry to be an interpolation.) But though it lacks the authority of the canonical writings, its true evangelical spirit and its earnest endeavours to promote the best interests of Christ's Church have secured it a place for ever among the most precious relics of Christian antiquity.

*

A word of warning must be added about Clement's quotations from Scripture. It is not only that he uses the Septuagint version, of which the text differs widely at times from our English Bibles. He also has a habit of presenting under the appearance of a continuous quotation a collection of extracts from various sources; and as these are sometimes loosely and inaccurately cited from memory, their identification is not always easy. On occasions, indeed, they are so unlike anything to be found in the known books of the Bible that despairing critics are reduced to supposing that Clement has taken them from some lost apocryphal source. (A good example of this is the long passage quoted in chapter viii, which some scholars take for a patchwork of Jeremiah, Isaiah, and the Psalms, while others hold it to be from an apocryphal addition to the book of Ezekiel!) In these circumstances I hope I may be pardoned for not indicating the origins of the numerous quotations in which Clement indulges, and leaving the reader free to exercise his own ingenuity instead.

From the colony of the Church
of God at ROME[1]

> *To the colony of the Church of God at* CORINTH, *called and sanctified by the will of God through our Lord Jesus Christ.*

All grace and peace to you from God
Almighty, through Jesus Christ.

THE CORINTHIANS' PREVIOUS GOOD RECORD

1. Because of our recent series of unexpected misfortunes and set-backs,[2] my dear friends, we feel there has been some delay in turning our attention to the causes of dispute in your community. We refer particularly to the odious and unholy breach of unity among you, which is quite incompatible with God's chosen people, and which a few hot-headed and unruly individuals have inflamed to such a pitch that your venerable and illustrious name, so richly deserving of everyone's affection, has been brought into serious disrepute.

There was a time when nobody could spend even a short while among you without noticing the excellence and constancy of your faith. Who ever failed to be impressed by your sober and selfless Christian piety, to tell of your generous spirit of hospitality,[3] or to pay tribute to the wide range and soundness of your knowledge? It was your habit at all times to act without fear or favour, living by the laws of God and deferring with correctness to those who were set over you.[4] Your elders were treated with the honour due to them; your young men were counselled to be soberly and seriously minded; your womenfolk were bidden to go about their duties in irreproachable devotion and purity of conscience, showing all proper affection to their husbands; they were taught to make obedience the rule of their lives, to manage their households decorously, and to be patterns of discretion in every way.

2. Humility, too, and a complete absence of self-assertion were common to you all; you preferred to offer submission rather than extort it, and giving was dearer to your hearts than receiving.

23

Asking no more than what Christ had provided for your journey through life, you paid careful heed to His words, treasured them in your hearts, and kept His sufferings constantly before your eyes. The reward was a deep and shining peace, a quenchless ardour for well-doing, and a rich outpouring of the Holy Spirit upon you all. You were full of aspirations to holiness; after any involuntary transgression you would stretch out suppliant hands to Almighty God in an agony of piety and devout trustfulness, and implore His mercy. Day and night you would wrestle on behalf of all the brotherhood, that in His mercy and compassion the whole number of His elect might be saved. In your single-minded innocence you harboured no resentments; any kind of faction or schism was an abomination to you. You mourned for a neighbour's faults, and regarded his failings as your own. Never did you grudge a kindly action; always you were ready for any deed of goodness. In the beauty of a pure and heavenly citizenship, whatever you did was done in the fear of God, and the statutes and judgments of the Lord were engraved on the tables of your hearts.

THE SINFULNESS OF JEALOUSY

3. But when good repute and rising numbers were granted to you in full measure, the saying of Scripture came to pass : *my beloved did eat and drink, he grew and waxed fat and kicked.* Envy and jealousy sprang up, strife and dissension, aggression and rioting, scuffles and kidnappings. Men of the baser sort rose up against their betters : the rabble against the respectable, folly against wisdom, youth against its elders. And now all righteousness and peace among you is at an end. Everywhere men are renouncing the fear of God; the eye of faith has grown dim, and instead of following the commandments, and living as becomes a citizen of Christ, each one walks after the desires of his own wicked heart. All have fallen back into the horrid sin of Envy – the sin that brought death into the world.

4. For what Scripture says is this : *After some days Cain brought an offering to God of the produce of the earth, and*

Abel brought of the firstlings of his flock and their fatness. The Lord took a favourable view of Abel and his gifts, but ignored Cain and his offering. At this Cain took offence, and his face grew black. 'Why are you so put out?' the Lord asked him; 'why so crestfallen? You were right to bring me an offering, but wrong in the decision you made. Was that not a sin? Not another word; he shall turn to you, and you shall have the mastery over him.' Cain said to his brother Abel, 'Let us go out to the open country'; and when they were out in the open, Cain fell upon his brother Abel and slew him. So you see, my friends, how envy and jealousy brought about the murder of a brother. Also, it was jealousy that made our father Jacob[5] take flight from the presence of his brother Esau. Jealousy, again, all but hounded Joseph to death, and brought him into servitude. Moses, because of jealousy, had to flee from Pharaoh king of Egypt, after he had heard one of his own fellow-countrymen say, *Who made you our judge and arbiter? Are you meaning to kill me as you killed the Egyptian yesterday?* Aaron and Miriam were expelled from the camp for being jealous. Jealousy brought down Dathan and Abiram to a living death for their rebellion against Moses the servant of God. Jealousy prompted the other tribes' envy of David, as well as his persecution by Israel's king Saul.

5. Leave these instances from the past, and come to some of the heroes of more recent times. Take the noble figures of our own generation. Even the greatest and most virtuous pillars of our Church were assailed by envy and jealousy, and had to keep up the struggle till death ended their days. Look at the holy Apostles. It was by sinful jealousy that Peter was subjected to tribulation, not once or twice but many times; it was in that way that he bore his witness, ere he left us for his well-earned place in glory. And Paul, because of jealousy and contention, has become the very type of endurance rewarded. He was in bonds seven times, he was exiled, he was stoned. He preached in the East and in the West, winning a noble reputation for his faith. He taught righteousness to all the world; and after reaching the furthest limits of the West,[6] and bearing his testimony before kings and rulers, he passed out of this world and was received

into the holy places. In him we have one of the greatest of all examples of endurance.

6. Besides these men of saintly life, there are many more of the elect who have undergone hardships and torments instigated by jealousy, and provide admirable object lessons for ourselves. There were women, hounded by jealousy to appear as Danaids and Dirces,[7] who endured fearful and diabolical tortures; yet in spite of their bodily frailty they finished the race of faith unshaken, and received their noble reward. Jealousy has estranged wives and their husbands, confounding the saying of our father Adam that *this is now bone of my bone and flesh of my flesh.* Envy and jealousy have even overthrown great cities, and uprooted mighty nations.

IT IS NEVER TOO LATE TO REPENT

7. Now, all this is not being written as a warning to you alone, my dear friends, but for a reminder to ourselves as well, because we too are in the same arena and have the same conflict before us. So let us be done with these barren and vapid fancies, and turn instead to the honourable, holy Rule of our tradition, so that we can find out what is good and pleasing and acceptable in the sight of Him who made us. Let us fix our thoughts on the Blood of Christ; and reflect how precious that Blood is in God's eyes, inasmuch as its outpouring for our salvation has opened the grace of repentance to all mankind. For we have only to survey the generations of the past to see that in every one of them the Lord has offered the chance of repentance to any who were willing to turn to Him. When Noah preached repentance, those who gave heed to him were saved. When, after Jonah had proclaimed destruction to the people of Nineveh, they repented of their sins and made atonement to God with prayers and supplications, they obtained their salvation, notwithstanding that they were strangers and aliens to Him.

8. All those who were ministers of the grace of God have spoken, through the Holy Spirit, of repentance. The very Lord of all Himself has spoken of it, and even with an oath. *By my*

life, the Lord declares, it is not the sinner's death that I desire, so much as his repentance; and He adds this gracious pronouncement, *Repent, O house of Israel, and turn from your wickedness. Say to the children of my people, Though your sins may stretch from earth to heaven, and though they may be redder than scarlet and blacker than sackcloth, yet if you turn wholeheartedly to me and say 'Father', I will listen to you as I would to a people that was holy.* And He says somewhere else, *Wash yourselves, and be clean; put away the evil of your souls from my eyes. Leave off your wickedness, and learn to do right. Seek justice, relieve the oppressed, do right by the fatherless, act fairly to the widow. Come, let us reason together, says the Lord; though your sins are crimson-red, I will make them as white as snow; though they are like scarlet, I will make them white as wool. If you are willing, and listen to me, you shall eat the good of the land; but if you refuse, and will not listen, a sword shall devour you. These words are from the Lord's own mouth.* Thus, by His own almighty will, He has confirmed His desire that repentance should be open to every one of His beloved.

THE EXEMPLARY OBEDIENCE OF THE SAINTS

9. Let us bow, then, to that sovereign and glorious will. Let us entreat His mercy and goodness, casting ourselves upon His compassion and wasting no more energy in quarrels and a rivalry which only ends in death. Consider some of those who have served His glorious majesty most perfectly. Take Enoch, for example; he was found righteous because of his obedience, and so he was translated, and for him there was no death. Or consider how, when Noah's duteous service had proved him faithful, he thereby became the herald of a new birth for the world; and by his means, too, the Lord preserved the brute creation which had entered in perfect amity together into the Ark.

10. Abraham, who was named the Friend, showed his loyalty by obeying the voice of God. At the call of obedience he quitted his own country and his kindred and his father's house, leaving behind him a petty region, an insignificant family, and a scanty

household in order to become an inheritor of the promises of God. For God's word to him had been, *Remove from your country and your kindred and your father's house, into a land that I will show you, and I will make you into a mighty nation. I will bless you, and make your name great, and you will be blessed. Those who bless you, I will bless, and curse those who curse you; and through you, every tribe on earth will be blessed.* And later, at his parting from Lot, God said to him, *Lift up your eyes, and look around you, from the spot where you are standing, to the north and south and east and west. All the land that you can see, I will give to you and your descendants for ever. I will make your offspring like the dust of the earth; the full sum of your descendants will only be reckoned if a man could number the very dust of the earth.* Further on, it says, *God brought out Abraham and said, Look up at the sky, and tell, if you can, the number of the stars; for even thus shall your posterity be. And Abraham believed God, and that was credited to him for righteousness.* It was also because of his faith and his hospitality that a son was given to him in his old age; and this son his obedience afterwards led him to offer up as a sacrifice to God, on the mountain which He had showed him.

11. Lot, for his hospitality[8] and his piety, was brought safely out of Sodom, when fire and brimstone were raining down in judgement on all the region round about. Moreover, on that occasion the Lord made it plain that, while He never forsakes those who place their hopes in Him, He visits pains and penalties on the rebellious; and as a sign of this, Lot's wife, who had accompanied him in his flight, but later changed her mind and fell out with him, was turned into a pillar of salt to this day. That was to let all men see how doubt and distrust of God's power bring a judgement upon themselves, and become a warning to future generations.

12. Rahab the harlot owed her preservation to her faith and hospitality. When Joshua the son of Nun sent his spies to Jericho, the king of the land discovered that they had come to spy out his territory, and sent men to seize them, so that they could be captured and put to death. But the hospitable Rahab took them in,

and hid them upstairs under some stalks of flax. When the king's agents arrived they said, 'The spies who are exploring our land came in here to you. Fetch them out; it is an order from the king.' 'Yes,' she answered, 'the men you are after did come to me; but they left again immediately. They have taken to the road,' she told them, pointing in the opposite direction. Later, she said to the others, 'I know for sure that the Lord God is delivering our land over to you, for dread and terror of you have fallen on the inhabitants; but when the time comes for you to take it, pray spare me and my father's household.' They replied, 'It shall be as you say. When you hear of our approach, get all your kinsfolk together under your own roof, and they will be safe. But any who are found outside the house will be put to death.' They went on to give her a sign, telling her she was to hang out a scarlet cord from her house – thereby typifying the redemption which all who put their trust and hope in God shall find, through the blood of the Lord. (Notice, dear friends, how in this woman there was not only faith, but prophecy also.)

AN APPEAL TO RENOUNCE OBSTINACY AND SCHISM

13. My brothers, do let us have a little humility; let us forget our self assertion and braggadocio and stupid quarrelling, and do what the Bible tells us instead. The Holy Spirit says, *The wise man is not to brag of his wisdom, nor the strong man of his strength, nor the rich man of his wealth; if a man must boast, he should boast of the Lord, seeking him out and acting with justice and uprightness.* More particularly, let us remember what the Lord Jesus Christ said in one of His lessons on mildness and forbearance. *Be merciful*, He told us, *that you may obtain mercy; forgive, that you may be forgiven. What you do yourself, will be done to you; what you give, will be given to you; as you judge, so you will be judged; as you show kindness, so it will be shown to you. Your portion will be weighed out for you in your own scales.* May this precept, and these commands, strengthen our resolve to live in obedience to His sacred words, and in humility of mind; for the Holy Word says, *Whom shall*

I look upon, but him that is gentle and peaceable, and trembles at my sayings?

14. It is surely more right and reverent for us, my brothers, to obey God than to follow people whose insolent unruliness has made them the ringleaders of this odious rivalry. It is no trifling risk that we run but on the contrary the most deadly peril, if we rashly lend ourselves to the designs of some who are plunging into strife and sedition to divert us from what is right. Rather let us show kindliness to one another, in the same sweet spirit of tenderness as our Maker. It is written, *the kind-hearted will inhabit the earth, and the innocent will remain upon it, but the transgressors will be rooted out of it*; and again, *I saw the ungodly soaring and shooting up like the cedars of Lebanon; but when I passed by again, lo and behold, he was gone, and when I searched for his place I could not discover it. Take good care of innocence, and keep your eyes on what is right; for a man of peace shall leave a posterity to follow him.*

15. Let us ally ourselves, then, with those who work for peace out of genuine devotion, and not with men who only pay lip service to it. There is a text in Scripture that says, *These people honour me with their lips, but their heart is far from me*; and again, *Blessings are in their mouth, but curses in their heart.* It also says, *They spoke to him with the lips of lovers, and their tongues uttered feigned vows; but their heart was not straight with him, nor did they keep faith with his covenant.* And for that reason, *Let the lying lips be struck dumb that speak wickedly against the righteous*; and furthermore, *May the Lord destroy all lying lips, and the braggart tongue, and those who say, We will enlarge our tongues; our lips belong to ourselves; who is lord over us? Because of the misery of the poor and the lamentations of the needy, I will rise up now, says the Lord, and place him in security; I will show myself bold in his defence.*

THE HUMILITY OF CHRIST AND THE SAINTS

16. Christ belongs to the lowly of heart, and not to those who would exalt themselves over His flock. The coming of our Lord

Jesus Christ, the Sceptre of God's Majesty, was in no pomp of pride and haughtiness – as it could so well have been – but in self-abasement, even as the Holy Ghost had declared of Him, saying, *Lord, who has believed what we have heard, and to whom has the Divine arm been revealed? For we proclaimed before the Lord that he resembles a babe in arms, or a root in waterless soil; there is not a trace of shapeliness or splendour about him. We saw him, and he had neither comeliness nor beauty; his appearance was mean, and inferior to that of other men. He was familiar with hard labour and the lash, and schooled to endure weakness; for he kept his face averted, and was despised and disregarded. Yet this is he who carries the burden of our sins, and suffers pain on our behalf. We took him for a man whose lot was toil and blows and indignities; but it was for our sins that he was wounded, and for our iniquities that he was afflicted. The chastisement that bought our peace fell upon him, and by his bruises we were healed. All of us went astray like sheep, each man taking his own wrong path; and for our sins the Lord delivered him up. Through all his ill-treatment he never opened his mouth; he was led away like a sheep to be slaughtered, and like a lamb that is mute before its shearer he never opened his lips. His sentence was to be humiliated; no one will ever recount his descendants, for his life was destroyed from off the earth. He has gone to his death for the transgressions of my people; and in requital for his burial I will give wicked men,[9] and men of wealth for his death, because he did no wrong, and no deceit was found in his mouth. It is the Lord's intention to cleanse him of his weals; and if you make an offering for your sins, your soul shall see your posterity living to a ripe old age. It is the Lord's intention to curtail the labours of his life, to show him light, to mould him with under-standing, and to vindicate him as a righteous man and a good servant to the many whose sins he shall bear in his own person. Men in plenty shall be given him for his portion, and he shall divide the spoils of the strong, because his life was delivered over to death, and he was counted among the transgressors. On his own shoulders he bore the sins of many, and for their sins he was delivered up.* Elsewhere, too, it says, *I am a worm, and no man; a public reproach, and an object of contempt to the people. All who saw me derided me; they spoke with their lips, nodding their heads and saying, He set his hopes on the Lord; let him deliver him, let him save him, since he has such a liking for him.*

You see, dear friends, what an example we have been given. If the Lord humbled Himself in this way, what ought we to do, who through Him have come under the yoke of His grace?

17. Let us take pattern by those who *went about in sheepskins and goatskins*[10] heralding the Messiah's coming; that is to say, Elijah and Elisha and Ezekiel among the prophets, and other famous names besides. Abraham, for instance, has great things said about him; he is even named the Friend of God; and yet, when he looks upon the glory of God, he acknowledges with humility, *I am dust and ashes.* It is also written of Job that *Job was upright and faultless, true and God-fearing, and kept himself from all evil;* but he too exclaims in self-reproach, *No man can be wholly pure from defilement, even if his life is but a single day long.* Moses was called *faithful in all his house,* and by his ministry God brought down plagues and torments in judgement upon Egypt; yet even he, though so greatly honoured, never indulged in high-flown speeches, but merely said when he received the Message out of the Bush, *Who am I, that you should send me? My voice is feeble, and my tongue is slow;* and on another occasion, *I am but smoke from a pot.*

18. And what of the illustrious figure of David? Though God says of him, *I have found a man after my own heart, even David the son of Jesse, and I have anointed him with everlasting mercy,* yet this is how he addresses God: *O God, in your great mercy have mercy on me; in the fullness of your compassion blot out my transgressions. Wash me clean of my wickedness, and pure of my sin. I know my own disobedience; my sin is always before my eyes. It was against you alone that I sinned, and did what was wrong in your sight; so that you may be proved right in your statements, and be acquitted when they impeach you. Look, I was conceived in iniquity, and my mother brought me forth in sin. But you loved truth, and showed me*

*the hidden secrets of your wisdom. You will sprinkle me with
hyssop, and I shall be made clean; you will wash me, and I
shall be made whiter than snow. You will bring sounds of joy
and exultation to my ears, and my bones, though humiliated,
will rejoice. Hide your face from my sins, and blot out all my
iniquities. Create a clean heart in me, O God; set a new spirit
of uprightness in me. Do not send me away from your
presence, or withdraw your holy spirit from me. Give me back
the joy of your salvation again; make me strong with your
sovereign spirit. Then I will teach your ways to the lawless,
and the wicked will turn back to you once more. Save me from
the guilt of blood, O God, God of my salvation, and my tongue
will exult over your righteousness. O Lord, you shall open my
mouth, and my lips will proclaim your praise. If you had wished
for a sacrifice, I would have given it; but burnt offerings will be
no pleasure to you. God's sacrifice is a broken spirit; God will
not scorn a broken and humbled heart.*

HARMONY AND COOPERATION ARE LESSONS WHICH NATURE ITSELF TEACHES US

19. Now it is not we alone who have been made better men by
the self-effacement and humble submissiveness of all these
famous personages, but generations of our predecessors as well,
and indeed everyone who has ever received the utterances of
God in fear and truth. Thus there exists a vast heritage of
glorious achievements for us to share in. Let us then make haste
and get back to the state of tranquillity which was set before us
in the beginning as the mark for us to aim at. Let us turn our
eyes to the Father and Creator of the universe, and when we
consider how precious and peerless are His gifts of peace, let us
embrace them eagerly for ourselves. Let us contemplate Him with
understanding, noting with the eyes of the spirit the patient forbearance that is everywhere willed by Him, and the total absence
of any friction that marks the ordering of His whole creation.

20. The heavens, as they revolve beneath His government, do
so in quiet submission to Him. The day and the night run the

course He has laid down for them, and neither of them interferes with the other. Sun, moon, and the starry choirs roll on in harmony at His command, none swerving from its appointed orbit. Season by season the teeming earth, obedient to His will, causes a wealth of nourishment to spring forth for man and beast and every living thing upon its surface, making no demur and no attempt to alter even the least of His decrees. Laws of the same kind sustain the fathomless deeps of the abyss and the untold regions of the underworld. Nor does the illimitable basin of the sea, gathered by the operations of His hand into its various different centres, overflow at any time the barriers encircling it, but does as He has bidden it – for His word was, *Thus far shall you come; at this point shall your waves be broken within you.* The impassable Ocean and all the worlds that lie beyond it[11] are themselves ruled by the like ordinances of the Lord. Spring, summer, autumn and winter succeed one another peaceably; the winds fulfil their punctual duties, each from its own quarter, and give no offence; the ever-flowing streams, created for our well-being and enjoyment, offer their breasts unfailingly for the life of man; and even the minutest of living creatures mingle together in peaceful accord. Upon all of these the great Architect and Lord of the universe has enjoined peace and harmony, for the good of all alike, but pre-eminently for the good of ourselves who have sought refuge in His mercies through our Lord Jesus Christ. To Him be glory and majesty for ever and ever, amen.[12]

21. Take care then, my friends, lest, if we fail to conduct ourselves worthily of Him and to do what is good and acceptable to Him in amity together, all this beneficence of His should turn to our condemnation. *The spirit of the Lord*, as the Bible tells us, *is a candle searching the inward parts of the body*; so let us keep in mind this nearness of His presence, remembering that not a single one of our thoughts or reasonings can ever be hidden from Him. The right thing, then, is not to run away from His will (for rather than oppose God, we had much better oppose the folly and senselessness of these self-important men and the bluster of their arrogant speeches), but to reverence the Lord Jesus Christ whose blood was given for us. Accordingly, let

us be respectful to those who have been set over us, honour our elders, and train up our young people in the fear of God; let us set our womenfolk on the road to goodness, by teaching them to be examples of lovable purity, to display real sincerity in their submissiveness, to prove the self-restraint of their tongues by observing silence, and to bestow equal affection, with no favouritism and as becomes holiness, upon all God-fearing persons. As for our children, see that they have their share of Christian instruction; let them learn how greatly a humble spirit avails with God, how mightily a chaste and innocent love prevails with Him, and how great and goodly a thing is the fear of Him, by which all who pass their lives therein with holiness and purity of heart are made sure of salvation. For He is the searcher of our thoughts and desires; His is the breath that is in us, and at His own good pleasure will He take it away.

22. All these promises find their confirmation when we believe in Christ, for it is He Himself who summons us, through His Holy Spirit, with the words, *Come, my children; listen to me, and I will teach you the fear of the Lord. Whose heart is set on a long life and days of happiness? Keep your tongue free of evil, and your lips from uttering deceit; turn away from wrong, and do what is good; seek peacefulness, and make that your aim. The Lord's eyes are on the righteous, and His ears open to their prayers; but the face of the Lord is against evil-doers, to blot out the memory of them from the earth. When a good man cries, the Lord listens, and delivers him from all his troubles. Also, the sinner will have scourgings in plenty, but mercy will enfold those who set their hopes on the Lord.*

THERE ARE NO GROUNDS FOR DOUBTING THE RESURRECTION

23.[13] The all-merciful and beneficent Father is compassionate to those that fear Him; to approach Him in sincerity of heart is to be repaid with His kind and gracious favours. So let us be done with vacillation, and indulge no more inward doubts of the reality of His great and glorious gifts. Far be from us those words of Scripture: *How miserable are the irresolute and they of a doubting heart, who say, Even in the time of our fathers we heard of these things; but see, we have grown old by now, and yet not one of them has happened to us.* Consider a tree, you unwise ones, and how apt a figure of yourselves it is. Look at the vine; it first casts its foliage, and then a bud appears, and next a leaf, and later a flower, and after that a young unripe grape, and then finally the full cluster. See how short a time it takes for the fruit to mature. Truly, His purpose will accomplish itself just as swiftly and suddenly; as indeed we have Scripture's own testimony, which says, *He will surely come quickly, he will not delay*; and again, *with no warning the Lord, the Holy One you are expecting, will come to his temple.*

24. Think, my dear friends, how the Lord offers us proof after proof that there is going to be a resurrection, of which He has made Jesus Christ the first-fruits by raising Him from the dead. My friends, look how regularly there are processes of resurrection going on at this very moment. The day and the night show us an example of it; for night sinks to rest, and day arises; day passes away, and night comes again. Or take the fruits of the earth; how, and in what way, does a crop come into being? When the sower goes out and drops each seed into the ground, it falls to the earth shrivelled and bare, and decays; but presently the power of the Lord's providence raises it from decay, and from that single grain a host of others spring up and yield their fruit.

25. Look at that strange portent that occurs in the East (in the neighbourhood of Arabia, to be precise). There is a bird known as a Phoenix, which is the only specimen of its kind and has a life of five hundred years. When the hour of its dissolution and death approaches, it makes a nest for itself out of frankincense and myrrh and other fragrant spices, and in the fullness of time it enters into this and expires. Its decaying flesh breeds a small grub, which is nourished by the moisture of the dead bird and presently grows wings. This, on reaching full growth, takes up the nest containing the bones of its predecessor and carries them all the way from the land of Arabia into Egypt, to the city

called Heliopolis. There, in the full light of day and before the eyes of all beholders, it flies to the altar of the Sun, deposits them there, and speeds back to its homeland; and when the priests consult their time records, they find that its arrival has marked the completion of the five-hundredth year.[14]

26. Now, when the Creator of all things has even made use of a bird to disclose the magnitude of His promises to us, need we find it such a great wonder that He has a resurrection in store for those who have served Him in holiness and in the confidence of a sound faith? For in Scripture we read, *You will raise me up, and I will praise you*; and also, *After I had lain down and fallen asleep, I rose up again; for you are with me.* Job too, says, *You will raise up this flesh of mine which has had all these trials to endure.*

27. Seeing then that we have this hope, let us knit fast our souls to Him who is ever true to His word and righteous in His judgements. He who has forbidden us to use any deception can much less be a deceiver Himself; untruth is the only thing that is impossible to God. So let us rekindle the ardour of our belief in Him, and also remind ourselves that there is nothing in the world with which He is not in close touch. With the word of His greatness has He assembled all that exists, and with a word He is able to overturn it again; for *who can say to him, What have you done? or who shall withstand the power of his might?* He will act at all times as, and when, He chooses; and not one of His decrees shall fail. The entire universe lies open before Him; and there is nothing that is hidden from His counsel; for *the heavens are a proclamation of God's glory, and the firmament a declaration of his handiwork. Day utters the message to day, and night to night proclaims the knowledge though there are no words or speeches and their voices are inaudible.*

AN EXHORTATION TO AMENDMENT OF LIFE

28. Therefore, since there is nothing He does not see and hear, let us approach Him with awe, and have done with this hateful fondness for mischief-making, so that we may find shelter in His

mercy from the judgement to come. For where can any of us flee to, from His mighty hand; or what sort of world will receive one who is a fugitive from Him? As it says in the Psalms,[15] *Whither shall I go, and where shall I hide, from your presence? If I climb up to heaven, you are there; if I retire to the ends of the earth, your right hand is there; if I make my bed in the pit, there is your Spirit.* Where then is there for a man to go, or where can he elude One whose grasp is all-encompassing?

29. It follows that we must approach Him in holiness of spirit, lifting up pure and undefiled hands to Him in love for the gracious and compassionate Father who has chosen us to be His own – for is it not written that *when the Most High divided up the peoples, and scattered the sons of Adam, he fixed the boundaries of the nations in accordance with the number of the angels of God;*[16] *but his people Jacob became the Lord's own portion, and Israel the land assigned to himself.* And it says somewhere else, *Behold, the Lord takes a people for himself out of the midst of the nations, as a man takes the first-fruits of his threshing floor; and it is out of that people that the Holy of Holies shall come.*

30. Since then we are the Holy One's own special portion, let us omit no possible means of sanctification. We must bid farewell to all slandering, lewd and unclean coupling, drinking and rioting, vile lusting, odious fornicating, and the pride which is an abomination. *God*, it says, *opposes the proud, but he gives grace to the humble*; so let us attach ourselves firmly to men who have received this grace. Let us clothe ourselves in a mutual tolerance of one another's views, cultivating humility and self-restraint, avoiding all gossiping and backbiting, and earning our justification by deeds and not by words. For it says, *he who is full of words shall be answered in full measure. Does a man think himself righteous for his much speaking? A short life is a blessing to any man born of woman;*[17] *never be prodigal of words.* Let any commendation of us proceed from God, and not from ourselves, for self-praise is hateful to God. Testimony to our good deeds is for others to give, as it was given to those righteous men who were our forefathers. Self-assertion, self-assurance, and a

bold manner are the marks of men accursed of God; it is those who show consideration for others, and are unassuming and quiet, who win His blessing.

31. Let us be intent on this blessing, then, and see which roads can lead us to it. Turn the early pages of history; what was it that caused our father Abraham to be blessed? Was it not his faith, which prompted him to acts of righteousness and truth? And it was Isaac's confident faith in what would follow that stretched him on the altar with a light heart. As for Jacob, who so submissively quitted his own country on account of his brother and came and served Laban, he was rewarded with the headship of the twelve tribes of Israelites.

32. Now, anyone who honestly examines each of these instances will perceive the magnitude of the gifts which God bestows. For it is from Jacob that all the priests and Levites who minister at God's altar have since descended. From him, too, according to the flesh, has come the Lord Jesus. From him there have issued kings and princes and rulers, in the line of descent from Judah; while the other chiefdoms which also sprang from him have their own no small claim to fame – as God promised when he said, *your posterity will be like the stars of heaven*. On all of these great honour and renown were bestowed; yet not for their own sakes, or because of their own achievements, or for the good works they did, but by the will of God. Similarly we also, who by His will have been called in Christ Jesus, are not justified by ourselves or our own wisdom or understanding or godliness, nor by such deeds as we have done in holiness of heart, but by that faith through which alone Almighty God has justified all men since the beginning of time. Glory be to Him for ever and ever, amen.

FAITH, HOWEVER, MUST BE ACCOMPANIED BY WORKS

33. What must we do, then, my brothers? Should we relax our efforts at well-doing, and cease to exercise Christian love? God forbid that we, at least, should ever come to such a pass. On the

contrary, let us be earnestly, even passionately, eager to set about any kind of activity that is good. Even the Architect and Lord of the universe Himself takes a delight in working. In His supreme power He has established the heavens, and in His unsearchable wisdom set them in order. He divided the earth from the waters around it, and settled it securely on the firm foundation of His will, and at His word He called to life the beasts of the field that roam its surface. He formed the sea and its creatures, and confined them by His power. Above all, with His own sacred and immaculate hands he fashioned man, who in virtue of his intelligence is the chiefest and greatest of all His works and the very likeness of His own image; for God said, *Let us make man in our image and likeness; and God created man, male and female he created them*. And when He had made an end of all His works, He gave them His approval and His blessing, saying, *Increase and multiply*. We see, then, that good works have not only embellished the lives of all just men, but are an adornment with which even the Lord has delighted to deck Himself; and therefore, with such an example before us, let us spare no effort to obey His will, but put all our energies into the work of righteousness.

34. A good workman can accept the reward of his labour with assurance, but one who is idle and shiftless cannot look his employer in the face. That is why we must devote ourselves heart and soul to the task of well-doing, for everything comes from the hand of God and He has already warned us, *See, the Lord is approaching, with his reward before him, to pay every man as his work deserves.* That is why He bids us believe Him implicitly and never be slothful or remiss over any good work. So now do let us place all this boasting and confidence of ours in Him, and submit ourselves to His will. Think of the vast company of His angels, who all wait on Him to serve His wishes. *Ten thousand times ten thousand stood before him*, says Scripture, *and thousand thousands did him service, crying, Holy, holy, holy is the Lord of hosts; all creation is full of his glory.* In the same way ought we ourselves, gathered together in a conscious unity, to cry to Him as it were with a single voice, if we

are to obtain a share of His glorious great promises – for it says that *no eye has seen, no ear has heard, no mortal heart has dreamed of the things God has in store for those who wait patiently for him.*

35. How blessed, how marvellous are the gifts of God, my friends! Some of them, indeed, already lie within our comprehension – the life that knows no death, the shining splendour of righteousness, the truth that is frank and full, the faith that is perfect assurance, the holiness of chastity – but what of the things prepared for those who wait? Who but the Creator and Father of eternity, the Most Holy Himself, knows the greatness and the beauty of these? Then let us strain every nerve to be found among those who wait in patience for Him, so that we too may earn a share of His promised gifts. And how is this to be done, my friends? Why, by fixing our minds trustfully on God; by finding out what is pleasing and acceptable to Him; by doing whatever agrees with His perfect will; by following the paths of truth. Wickedness and wrongdoing of every kind must be utterly renounced; all greed, quarrelling, malice and fraud, scandal-mongering and backbiting, enmity towards God, glorification of self, presumption, conceit, and want of hospitality; for men who do these things – and not only men who do them, but men who consent to them – are held in detestation by God. Scripture says, *But unto the wicked God says, Why do you recite my statutes and take my covenant upon your lips? You hated instruction; you flung my words behind you; when you saw a thief you went along with him, and you chose the company of adulterers. Your mouth abounded with evil, and your tongue wove a web of trickery. You sat there vilifying your brother and planning the downfall of your own mother's son. While you were doing all this I remained silent, and so you thought, you wicked man, that I was no better than yourself; but I will rebuke you, and make you see yourself as you are. Think of this, all you who forget God, or he will pounce on you like a lion, and there will be nobody to save you. It is the offering of praise that will glorify me; there lies the way by which I will show him God's salvation.*

41

36. And it is by that very way, dear friends, that we find our own salvation : even Jesus Christ, the High Priest by whom our gifts are offered, and the Protector by whom our feebleness is aided. Through Him we can look up to the highest heaven and see, as in a glass, the peerless perfection of the face of God. Through Him the eyes of our hearts are opened, and our dim and clouded understanding unfolds like a flower to the light; for through Him the Lord permits us to taste the wisdom of eternity. He is the splendour of God's majesty; and as much greater than the angels as the title He has inherited is a loftier one than theirs. For it is written, *He makes his angels into winds, and his servitors into a flame of fire, but of the Son the Lord declares, You are my son, this very day have I fathered you; ask of me, and I will give you nations for your inheritance and the furthest limits of the world for your possession.* Again, God says to Him, *Sit down at my right hand, until I make your enemies a cushion for your feet.* Who are those enemies? Why, wicked persons who set themselves against His will.

UNITY AND COOPERATION FOR THE COMMON GOOD

37. So now, my friends, let us get on resolutely with our warfare under His unerring directions. Think of the men who serve our own commanders in the field, and the prompt and orderly obedience with which they go about their duties. Not all of them are marshals, generals, colonels, captains, or the like; nevertheless, each at his own level executes the orders of the emperor and the military chiefs. For the great cannot exist without the small, nor the small without the great. Every organism is composed of various different elements; and this ensures its own good. Take the body as an instance; the head is nothing without the feet, nor are the feet anything without the head. Even the smallest of our physical members are necessary and valuable to the whole body; yet all of them work together and observe a common subordination, so that the body itself is maintained intact.

38. In Christ Jesus, then, let this corporate body of ours be likewise maintained intact, with each of us giving way to his

neighbour in proportion to our spiritual gifts. The strong are not to ignore the weak, and the weak are to respect the strong. Rich men should provide for the poor and the poor should thank God for giving them somebody to supply their wants. If a man is wise, let him show his wisdom by good deeds, not by words; and if he is modest, let him leave others to speak of his modesty, instead of proclaiming it himself. Also, one who is physically chaste must not brag of it, knowing that the ability to control his desires has been given him by Another. For just consider, my brothers, the original material from which we took our being. What were we, pray, and who were we, at the moment of our first coming into the world? Our Maker and Creator brought us out of darkness into His universe as it were out of a tomb; even before our birth He was ready with His favours for us. To Him we owe everything, and therefore on every count we are under the obligation to return thanks to Him. Glory be to Him for ever and ever, amen.

39. Men who have no intelligence or understanding, men who are without sense or instruction, make a mock of us and ridicule us, in their wish to raise themselves in their own esteem. But what is there that anyone who is mortal can really effect? What force is there in anyone born of this earth? It is written, *there was no shape that my eyes could see, yet I heard the breath of a whisper saying, What, can a mortal man be pure before the Lord? If he puts no trust in his own servants, and has found that even his angels can err, shall mere man escape reproach in his doings? Heaven itself is not clean in his sight; much less they who dwell in houses of clay – that very clay of which we ourselves are formed. Upon such he preys like a moth; between dawn and sunset they cease to be; they perish, with no power to help themselves. He breathes on them, and they are no more, for there is no wisdom in them. Call, now; and see if any will heed, or if any of the holy angels will appear to you. An unwise man's indignation is his ruin, and a senseless man's resentment*[18] *is death to him. I have seen fools putting down their roots, but very soon their house was swallowed up. Let there be no redress for their children; let them become a laughing-stock in the gates of lesser*

43

men, with none to come to their rescue. That which was prepared
for them shall the righteous consume, nor shall they themselves
be delivered from evil.

THE CHURCH'S LITURGY AND HIERARCHY ARE OF
DIVINE INSTITUTION, AND MUST BE RESPECTED

40. All these things are plain to us who have scanned the depths of sacred lore. It follows, then, that there ought to be strict order and method in our performance of such acts as the Master has prescribed for certain times and seasons. Now, it was His command that the offering of gifts and the conduct of public services should not be haphazard or irregular, but should take place at fixed times and hours. Moreover, in the exercise of His supreme will He has Himself declared in what place and by what persons He desires this to be done, if it is all to be devoutly performed in accordance with His wishes and acceptably to his will. Consequently, they who present their offerings at such appointed times are accepted and blessed, since the care with which they observe the Master's laws clears them of all offence. The High Priest, for example, has his own proper services assigned to him, the priesthood has its own station, there are particular ministries laid down for the Levites, and the layman[19] is bound by regulations affecting the laity.

41. In the same way, my brothers, when we offer our own Eucharist to God, each one of us should keep to his own degree. His conscience must be clear, he must not infringe the rules prescribed for his ministering, and he is to bear himself with reverence. The continual daily sacrifices, peace-offerings, sin-offerings and trespass-offerings are by no means offered in every place,[20] brothers, but at the altar in front of the Temple; and then only after a careful scrutiny of the offering by the High Priest and the other ministers aforesaid. Anything done otherwise than in conformity with God's will is punishable with death. Take note from this, my brothers, that since we ourselves have been given so much fuller knowledge, the peril that we incur is correspondingly graver.

42. Now, the Gospel was given to the Apostles for us by the Lord Jesus Christ; and Jesus the Christ was sent from God. That is to say, Christ received His commission from God, and the Apostles theirs from Christ. The order of these two events was in accordance with the will of God. So thereafter, when the Apostles had been given their instructions, and all their doubts had been set at rest by the resurrection of our Lord Jesus Christ from the dead, they set out in the full assurance of the Holy Spirit to proclaim the coming of God's kingdom. And as they went through the territories and townships preaching, they appointed their first converts – after testing them by the Spirit – to be bishops and deacons for the believers of the future. (This was in no way an innovation, for bishops and deacons had already been spoken of in Scripture long before that; there is a text that says, *I will confirm their bishops in righteousness, and their deacons in faith.*[21])

43. Does it surprise us that Christian men, entrusted by God with such a mission, should have made these appointments? Surely not, for the blessed Moses, *a servant faithful in all his house*, has set down fully in the sacred books the instructions which he himself received; and the other prophets also, who came after him, all bear their witness to the ordinances which he laid down. When a rivalry arose over the priesthood, and the tribes were disputing for the privilege of this honourable title, Moses ordered the twelve tribal chiefs to bring him their staves, each with the name of his tribe inscribed upon it. He took the staves, bound them together, sealed them with the chiefs' own rings, and placed them on God's table in the Tabernacle of Witness. He shut the doors of the Tabernacle, and sealed the keys in the same way as the staves. 'Now, men and brethren', he told them, 'the tribe whose staff shall blossom is the one God has chosen to serve Him in the priesthood'. Next morning he called Israel together, all six hundred thousand of them, and after showing the chieftains the seals, he opened the Tabernacle of Witness and took out the staves; whereupon the staff of Aaron was found to have borne not only blossoms, but fruit as well. What is the inference, my friends? Do you suppose Moses was

45

not well aware beforehand that this would be the result? Of course he was; but he took that way of avoiding disorders in Israel, so that the name of the one true God (to whom be glory for ever, amen) might be magnified.

44. Similarly, our Apostles knew, through our Lord Jesus Christ, that there would be dissensions over the title of bishop. In their full foreknowledge of this, therefore, they proceeded to appoint the ministers I spoke of, and they went on to add an instruction that if these should fall asleep, other accredited persons should succeed them in their office. In view of this, we cannot think it right for these men now to be ejected from their ministry, when, after being commissioned by the Apostles (or by other reputable persons at a later date) with the full consent of the Church, they have since been serving Christ's flock in a humble, peaceable and disinterested way, and earning everybody's approval over so long a period of time. It will undoubtedly be no light offence on our part, if we take their bishopric away from men who have been performing its duties with this impeccable devotion. How happy those presbyters must be who have already passed away, with a lifetime of fruitfulness behind them; they at least need fear no eviction from the security they are now enjoying! You, however, as we notice, in more than one instance have turned men out of an office in which they were serving honourably and without the least reproach.

OPPOSITION TO GOD'S MINISTERS IS IMPIOUS

45. By all means be pugnacious and hot-headed, my brothers, but about things that will lead to salvation. Just take a look at the sacred scriptures; they are the authentic voice of the Holy Spirit, and you know that they contain nothing that is contrary to justice, nor is anything in them falsified. You are not going to find men of piety evicting the righteous there. The righteous were indeed persecuted, but only by men who were wicked. It was impious men who threw them into prison; it was lawless men who stoned them; it was men in the grip of odious and

criminal jealousy who were their murderers. If that is not the case, my friends, what are we going to say? Shall we say that Daniel was cast into the lions' den by men who really had the fear of God in their hearts? Shall we say that Ananias, Azarias and Misael were shut up in the fiery furnace by men who were engaged in the honourable and illustrious service of the Most High? A thousand times no. Who, in fact, were the people who did such things? They were miscreants steeped in every kind of villainy; wrought up to such fury that they could deliver over to torments men who were piously and innocently bent on serving their God. Little did they guess that the Most High is the guardian and protector of all who serve His holy Name (glory to Him for ever, amen); because their victims, whose trusting endurance won them a heritage of honour and renown, are now exalted on high, and enrolled by God in His tablets of remembrance for all future ages; amen.

46. It is the example of such men as these, my brothers, that we must make our own. It is written, *Seek ye the company of the holy, for they who seek their company shall themselves be made holy*. And it says somewhere else, *With the innocent you shall be innocent, with the chosen you shall be chosen, with the wayward you shall be wayward*. So let us take the innocent and the upright for our companions, for it is they who are God's chosen ones. Why must there be all this quarrelling and bad blood, these feuds and dissensions among you? Have we not all the same God, and the same Christ? Is not the same Spirit of grace shed upon us all? Have we not all the same calling in Christ? Then why are we rending and tearing asunder the limbs of Christ, and fomenting discord against our own body? Why are we so lost to all sense and reason that we have forgotten our membership of one another? Remember the words of the Lord Jesus, how He said, *Woe to that man; it would have been a good thing for him if he had never been born, instead of upsetting one of my chosen ones. It would be better for him to be pitched into the sea with a millstone hung round him, than to lead a single one of my chosen astray*. Your disunity, however, has led many astray; and yet, in spite of the

discouragement and doubt it has sown in many minds and the distress it has brought upon us all, you still persist in your disaffection.

47. Read your letter from the blessed Apostle Paul again. What did he write to you in those early Gospel days? How truly the things he said about himself and Cephas and Apollos were inspired by the Spirit! – for even at that time you had been setting up favourites of your own. Such partiality was perhaps less culpable in those days, for two of the men you favoured were Apostles of the highest repute, and the third was one to whom they had themselves given their approval. But think of the persons who have seduced you now! They have lessened all respect for that much-vaunted fraternal affection of yours. It is shameful, my dear friends, shameful in the extreme, and quite unworthy of the Christian training you have had, that the loyal and ancient church of Corinth, because of one or two individuals, should now be reputed to be at odds with its clergy. Even those who do not share our faith have heard this report, as well as ourselves; so that your thoughtlessness has brought the name of the Lord into disrespect, to say nothing of imperilling your own souls.

THE BLESSEDNESS OF CHRISTIAN LOVE

48. There must be no time lost in putting an end to this state of affairs. We must fall on our knees before the Master and implore Him with tears graciously to pardon us, and bring us back again into the honourable and virtuous way of brothers who love one another. For that is the gateway of righteousness, the open gate to life; as it is written, *Open me the gate of righteousness, that I may go in and praise the Lord. This is the gate of the Lord; the righteous shall come in by it.* There are many gates standing open, but the *gate of righteousness* is the gate of Christ, where blessings are in store for every incomer who pursues the path of godliness and uprightness, and goes about his duties without seeking to create trouble. By all means let a man be a true believer, let him be capable of expounding

the secrets of revelation, and a judicious assessor of what he hears, and a pattern of virtue in all his doings. But the higher his reputation stands, so much the more humble-minded he ought to be; and furthermore, his eyes should be fixed on the good of the whole community rather than on his own personal advantage.

49. If there is true Christian love in a man, let him carry out the precepts of Christ. Who can describe the constraining power of a love for God? Its majesty and its beauty who can adequately express? No tongue can tell the heights to which love can uplift us. Love binds us fast to God. Love casts a veil over sins innumerable. There are no limits to love's endurance, no end to its patience. Love is without servility, as it is without arrogance. Love knows of no divisions, promotes no discord; all the works of love are done in perfect fellowship. It was in love that all God's chosen saints were made perfect; for without love nothing is pleasing to Him. It was in love that the Lord drew us to Himself; because of the love He bore us, our Lord Jesus Christ, at the will of God, gave His blood for us – His flesh for our flesh, His life for our lives.

50. See then, dear friends, what a great and wondrous thing love is. Its perfection is beyond all words. Who is fit to be called its possessor, but those whom God deems worthy? Let us beg and implore of His mercy that we may be purged of all earthly preferences for this man or that, and be found faultless in love. Though every generation from Adam to the present day has passed from the earth, yet such of them as by God's grace were perfected in love have their place now in the courts of the godly, and at the visitation of Christ's kingdom they will be openly revealed. For it is written, *Go into your secret chambers for a very little while, till my rage and my fury pass away; and then I will remember a day of gladness, and raise you out of your graves.* My friends, if we keep God's commandments in a true loving comradeship together, so that our sins may be forgiven for that love's sake, we are blessed indeed. It is written, *blessed are they whose iniquities are forgiven, and over whose sins a veil is drawn; blessed is the man of whose sins the Lord takes no account, and on whose lips there is no deceit.* And this blessing

was theirs who were chosen by God through Jesus Christ our Lord. To Him be glory for ever and ever, amen.

A FINAL APPEAL

51. So let us beg forgiveness for all our misdoings, and the wrongs which our Adversary's intervention has moved us to commit. Those who have taken the lead in promoting faction and discord should bethink themselves of that Hope which is common to us all. If men are really living in the fear and love of God, they would sooner endure affliction themselves than see their neighbours suffer, and would prefer reproach to fall on them rather than on the tradition of peaceful harmony which has been so proudly and loyally handed down to us. It is better for a man to admit his faults frankly than to harden his heart, as the hearts of those who rebelled against Moses the servant of God were hardened. The judgement of those men was made plain for all to see, for they went down to the grave alive, and *death shall be their shepherd*. Pharaoh, too, and his army, with all the chieftains of Egypt and their chariots and horsemen, were swallowed up in the Red Sea and perished, for no other reason than that their foolish hearts were hardened, after God's servant Moses had performed his signs and wonders in the land of Egypt.

52. My brothers, our Master is one to whom need of any sort is unknown. Nothing at all does He ask of anyone, save only frank confession to Himself. David, His own chosen, says, *I will confess to the Lord, and that will please him more than a young calf with horns and hooves. Let the poor see this, and be glad.* He also says, *Offer a sacrifice of praise to God, and pay your vows to the Most High; then call upon me in your hour of trouble, and I will deliver you, and you shall glorify me.* For *the sacrifice of God is a contrite spirit.*

53. You know the sacred scriptures, my friends; you know them well, and you have studied the Divine utterances. Therefore we write to remind you how, when Moses went up into the mountain and had spent forty days and forty nights in fast-

ing and self-abasement, God said to him, *Make haste and go down from here, for your people whom you brought out of Egypt have broken my law. They have very soon left the way you told them to follow, and have been making molten idols for themselves.* And the Lord went on, *More than once I have spoken to you and said, Look, I have seen this people, and they are stiff-necked. Now let me destroy them; I will wipe out their name from under heaven, and make you yourself into a wondrous great nation, far more numerous than they are.* But Moses replied, *No Lord, not so. Forgive this people their sin, or else blot me too out of the book of the living.* What immeasurable love! Perfection beyond compare! A minister speaking up boldly to his Lord and demanding pardon for the multitude, or his own destruction along with them!

54. Is there any man of noble mind among you? A man who is compassionate? A man overflowing with love? Then let such a one say, 'If it is I who am the cause of any disorder, friction, or division among you, I will remove myself. I will go away, anywhere you wish, and I will do anything the congregation says; only let there be peace between Christ's flock and their appointed clergy'. Anyone who does this will earn a great name for himself in Christ, and be sure of a welcome anywhere (for *the earth and everything in it is the Lord's*). Men who were truly citizens of heaven – the citizenship that brings no regrets – have done such things in the past, and they will still do so today.

55. Even among the heathen one can recall instances of this kind. Numerous kings and rulers, in times of pestilence, have offered themselves for death at the bidding of an oracle, to save their subjects at the cost of their own lives; numbers, again, have pronounced sentence of exile on themselves for the sake of allaying civil disturbances. As for our own people, we know that many have surrendered themselves to captivity as a ransom for others, and many more have sold themselves into slavery and given the money to provide others with food. Even females have frequently been enabled by God's grace to achieve feats of heroism. The blessed Judith, when her city was in a state of siege, begged permission from the elders to visit the enemy's camp;

and then, for love of her country and her beleaguered people, she took her life in her hands and went forth, and the Lord delivered Holofernes into the hands of a weak woman. Esther, too, in the fullness of her faith, took a similar risk to save the children of Israel from the destruction that was threatening them. In fasting and humiliation she made her supplication to the all-seeing Lord of eternity; and when He saw the humbleness of her spirit, He delivered the people for whom she had put herself in jeopardy.

56. On our part likewise, then, let us plead for those who have fallen from grace, that they may be given the unselfishness and the humility to surrender themselves, not indeed to us, but to the will of God. By so doing they may be sure of a full, fruitful and sympathetic remembrance before God and the congregation. O my friends, do let us accept correction; it is something nobody ought to resent. Mutual admonition is wholly good and beneficial, for it leads us into conformity with the will of God. The sacred word says, *the Lord chastised me severely, yet without delivering me to death. Those whom the Lord loves, he chastises; everyone whom he acknowledges as a son, he scourges.* It also says, *a righteous man will chastise me in mercy and reprove me; but may my head never be anointed with the oil of sinners.* And again it says, *Happy is the man whom the Lord reproves. Reject not the admonitions of the Almighty, for though he inflicts pain, yet afterwards he makes whole again; he wounds, but his hands bring healing. He will bring you out of six troubles, and in the seventh no ill will touch you. In famine he will save you from death, and in war he will rescue you from the edge of the sword. He will hide you from the lash of tongues, and when evils come upon you you shall not be afraid. You shall laugh at the wicked and the lawless; even the savage beasts will have no terrors for you, for you and the creatures of the wild will be at peace together. You will know then that your household can dwell in peace and your tent never lack for livelihood. You will know, too, that your descendants will be many, and your children like the lush growth of the meadows. And you will go to your grave like a*

*ripe sheaf which men gather in when its hour is come, or like
a heap of wheat all ready for the thresher.* So you see, my friends,
how ample a protection is assured to those whom the Master
chastises. He is a good Father, who chastens us that we may
find mercy through His holy correction.

57. Those of you, then, who were at the root of these disorders, pray now make your submission to the clergy. Bend
the knees of your hearts and accept correction, so that it may
bring you to a better frame of mind. Learn to subordinate yourselves; curb those loud and overbearing speeches. It will be
better for you to be lowly but respected members of Christ's
flock, than to be apparently enjoying positions of eminence but
in fact to be cast out from every hope of Him. In the Wisdom
of Perfection [22] it says, *See now, I am going to put before you
the utterance of my Spirit, and teach you my word. Because I
called you and you would not listen, because I uttered my words
and you would not attend, but made light of my counsels and
refused to heed my reproofs, therefore I will smile at your destruction. When ruin falls upon you and sudden confusion seizes
you, when calamity comes like a whirlwind, or tribulation and
siege overtake you, then I will exult. When you call upon me,
you will find that I shall not hear; the wicked will seek me and
will not find me, because they hated wisdom and rejected the
fear of the Lord; they would not listen to my advice, but
mocked at my reproof. Therefore they shall have the fruits of
their own way to eat, and be filled full with their own ungodliness. Because of the wrong they did to the innocent, they shall
be slain; examination of the ungodly shall spell destruction
for them. But he who listens to me shall dwell in the tents of
hope securely; he shall abide in peace, without fear of any evil
thing.*

58. Then let us show ourselves obedient to His all-holy and
glorious Name, so that we may escape the doom that was pronounced of old by Wisdom upon the ungodly, and may dwell
in trustful reliance on the most sacred Name of His majesty.
Be counselled by us, and you will have nothing to regret. As
surely as God lives, as Jesus Christ lives, and the Holy Ghost

also (on whom are set the faith and hope of God's elect), so surely the man who keeps the divinely appointed decrees and statutes with humility and an unfailing consideration for others, and never looks back, will be enrolled in honour among the number of those who are saved through Jesus Christ, by whom is God glorified for ever and ever, amen.

59. But if there are any who refuse to heed the declarations He has made through our lips, let them not doubt the gravity of the guilt and the peril in which they involve themselves. For our part we will take care to be innocent of any such offence; and we will entreat the Creator of all things with heartfelt prayer and supplication that the full sum of His elect, as it has been numbered throughout all the world, may ever be preserved intact through His beloved Son Jesus Christ, by whom He has called us out of darkness to light, and from ignorance to the clear knowledge of the glory of His name.

A LITURGICAL INTERCESSION

[Teach us, O Lord] [23] ... to hope in thy Name, which is the source and fount of all creation. Open the eyes of our hearts to know thee, who alone art Highest amid the highest, and ever abidest Holy amidst the holy. Thou dost bring down the haughtiness of the proud, and scatterest the devices of the people. Thou settest up the lowly on high, and the lofty thou dost cast down. Riches and poverty, death and life, are in thine hand; thou alone art the discerner of every spirit, and the God of all flesh. Thine eyes behold the depths and survey the works of man; thou art the aid of those in peril, the saviour of them that despair, the creator and overseer of everything that hath breath. By thee the nations of the earth are increased; and from all mankind thou hast chosen out such as love thee through thy dear child Jesus Christ, by whom thou hast taught us and raised us to sanctification and honour. Grant us, O Lord, we beseech thee, thy help and protection. Do thou deliver the afflicted, pity the lowly, raise the fallen, reveal thyself to the needy, heal the sick, and bring home thy wandering people.

Feed thou the hungry, ransom the captive, support the weak, comfort the faint-hearted. Let all the nations of the earth know that thou art God alone, that Jesus Christ is thy child, and that we are thy people and the sheep of thy pasture.

60. Thou, O Lord, by thine operations didst bring to light the everlasting fabric of the universe, and didst create the world of men. From generation to generation thou art faithful, righteous in judgement, wondrous in might and majesty. Wisely hast thou created, prudently hast thou established, all things that are. To look around is to see thy goodness; to trust in thee is to know thy loving kindness. O most Merciful, O most Pitiful, absolve us from our sins and offences, from our errors and our shortcomings. Lay not every sin of thy servants and handmaidens to their charge, but make us clean with the cleansing of thy truth. Direct thou our goings, till we walk in holiness of heart and our works are good and pleasing in thy sight and the sight of our rulers. Yea, Lord, show the light of thy countenance in peace upon us for our good; and so shall we be sheltered by thy mighty hand, and saved from all wrongdoing by thine out-stretched arm. Deliver us from such as hate us without a cause; to us and all mankind grant peace and concord, even as thou didst to our forefathers when they called devoutly upon thee in faith and truth; and make us to be obedient both to thine own almighty and glorious Name and to all who have the rule and governance over us upon earth.

61. For it is thou, O Master, who in thy supreme and ineffable might hast given to them their sovereign authority; to the intent that we, acknowledging the glory and honour thou hast bestowed upon them, should show them all submission. Grant unto them then, O Lord, health and peace, harmony and security, that they may exercise without offence the dominion which thou hast accorded them. And forasmuch, O heavenly Master and Monarch eternal, as thou dost thus give to the sons of men glory and honour and power over the dwellers upon earth, vouchsafe so to direct their counsels as may be good and pleasing in thy sight, that in peace and mildness they may put to godly use the authority thou hast given them, and so find

mercy with thee. To thee, who alone canst grant to us these and other yet more excellent benefits, we offer up our praises through Jesus Christ, the High Priest and Guardian of our souls; through whom be glory and majesty unto thee now and for all generations and unto ages of ages. Amen.

EPILOGUE

62. Of what is due to our holy religion, and of the more useful aids to virtue for men who desire to advance in godliness and righteousness, we have now written enough to you, my brothers. Belief, repentance, true Christian love, self-discipline, discretion, perseverance – we have touched on these in all their aspects. We have reminded you of your duty to earn in all holiness the approval of Almighty God by a life of rectitude, truthfulness, and patient resignation, and to live amicably and without malice together, in peace and charity and unfailing consideration for others. This, as we have pointed out, is how our forefathers won approval, by the humility of their bearing towards God, their Father and Creator, and towards all their fellow-men. And we have been the more encouraged to lay these things before you, inasmuch as we knew we were addressing persons of faith and good repute, who have spent careful study on the maxims of the divine Teaching.

63. In view of the shining examples that have been set before us, then, it is a moral duty for us to bow the head and take our seat on the stool of submission; so that these fruitless differences may be composed, and our rightful destiny fulfilled without occasion for reproach. So you will afford us great joy and happiness if you will lay to heart what we have written through the Holy Spirit, and will respond to the appeal for peace and harmony which we have made in this letter, by putting an end once and for all to the rancours of an impious rivalry. We have sent envoys to you of trustworthiness and discretion, whose lives here among us have been irreproachable from youth to age; and they shall be witnesses between ourselves and you. Our purpose in so doing is to let you see that our whole concern has

been, and still is, for the speedy restoration of peace among you.

64. In conclusion, may the all-seeing God, the Ruler of spirits and Lord of all flesh, who has chosen the Lord Jesus Christ, and through Him ourselves to be a people for His possession, grant to every soul that is called by His glorious and holy Name such faith and fear, such peace and patience, such forbearance, self-restraint, purity and sobriety, that they may be pleasing to His Name; through our High Priest and Protector Jesus Christ, by whom be glory, majesty, might and honour to Him both now and for ever, world without end. Amen.

POSTSCRIPT

65. Make haste and send our messengers, Claudius Ephebus, Valerius Vito,[24] and Fortunatus, back to us in peace and joy; so that news of the truce and the unity for which we are praying and longing may reach us the more speedily, and we may the sooner rejoice over your return to order. The grace of our Lord Jesus Christ be with you, and with each and all everywhere whom God has called by Him; and through Him be glory and honour to God, with might, majesty, and everlasting dominion from all ages now and to eternity. Amen.

NOTES

1. Literally 'the Church of God which is transiently sojourning in Rome'. Clement is here using a technical term which denotes the temporary residents of a place, as distinct from its permanent inhabitants; for the Christian's true home is not on earth, but in heaven (cf. *Hebrews* xi, 13, 'strangers and pilgrims on the earth'). I have tried to express his idea by the word 'colony', in the sense in which we might speak of 'the French colony in London'.

2. The persecution of Christians which took place at Rome under Domitian in 93.

3. Corinth was a natural stopping-place for travellers between Rome and the East, and hospitality was much in request. The pointed

EARLY CHRISTIAN WRITINGS

allusions in this letter to the hospitable qualities of Abraham (ch. x), Lot (ch. xi), and Rahab (ch. xii), and the warning against inhospitality in ch. xxxv, suggest that the contemporary Corinthians were neglecting this Christian obligation.

4. The authorities of the Church, not the State.

5. Clement, the Greek-speaking Roman, writes as one of the true Israel.

6. The Pillars of Hercules (Straits of Gibraltar). It thus seems that St Paul's hopes of visiting Spain, of which he speaks in *Romans* xv, 24, must have been subsequently fulfilled.

7. If the text is genuine, this may be an allusion to the practice of compelling Christian victims to enact the parts of mythological characters in the arena.

8. In entertaining the angels (*Genesis* xix, 2, 3).

9. The wicked and the wealthy are to die in requital for His death.

10. The conventional dress of prophets.

11. The ancients frequently contemplate the possible existence of strange unknown lands beyond the setting sun (e.g. Plato's Atlantis).

12. Modern scholars describe this chapter as a free rendering, or paraphrase, of part of the primitive Roman Canon of the Mass (in which, however, the concept of Nature's universal orderliness is drawn from Greek philosophy).

13. Chapters 23–7 form a digression from the main theme of the letter, presumably suggested by the same kind of scepticism among the Corinthians as had inspired the famous fifteenth chapter of St Paul's first epistle to them.

14. The story of the Phoenix, which enjoyed wide credence in classical times, arises from the misinterpretation of an Egyptian hieroglyph indicating the periodic recurrence of some astronomical phenomenon. Here Clement makes the bird typical of the general resurrection of all believers, though later writers prefer a more specific application to the Person of Christ.

15. Literally 'the Writings', the general name for Old Testament books not included in the two divisions of the 'Law' and the 'Prophets'.

16. The Hebrew text from which our English Bible is translated mistakenly reads 'the children of Israel' instead of 'the angels of God'. Clement's quotation from the Septuagint preserves the true sense, which is that while the Gentile nations were given angels as their guardians, God reserved Israel under His own protection.

17. Since it provides less opportunity for talking too much.

18. Indignation ... resentment; i.e. against God.

19. Literally, 'the laic man'. This is the earliest occurrence of the word in any surviving Christian document. The Greek word *laos*, from which 'laic' derives, is an ecclesiastical term denoting the holy people of God, the congregation, as distinct from their clergy.

20. At first sight the use of the present tense seems to suggest that Clement was writing before the destruction of the Temple and the consequent cessation of its sacrifices in A.D. 70. Such an early date for the epistle, however, is not possible, so we must assume that he is simply quoting the Jewish regulations as they existed while they were still in force.

21. The Septuagint version of *Isaiah* lx, 17, is, 'I will give thy rulers in peace and thy overseers in righteousness'. By introducing the deacons we may suppose that Clement intends to bring out what he considers to be the true meaning of the prophecy.

22. This, literally 'the Wisdom comprising all virtues', is a title frequently given by early Christian writers to the Book of Proverbs, from the personified figure of Wisdom who speaks in the first chapter. (The books of Wisdom and Ecclesiasticus, in the Apocrypha, are also sometimes referred to by the same name.)

23. These words do not occur in the text, but some such addition is necessary to complete the sense.

24. As Nero belonged to the Claudian family, and his consort Messalina to the Valerian, several instances have been found of the two names Claudius (or Claudia) and Valerius (or Valeria) occurring in combination with reference to servants in the royal employment. Possibly this is the case here. It has even been conjectured that these two elderly envoys may have been among the members of 'Caesar's household' mentioned by St Paul in *Philippians* iv, 22.

*

THE EPISTLES OF
IGNATIUS

*

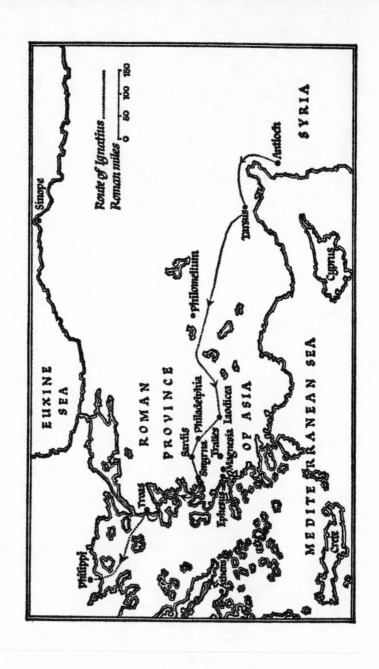

Ignatius of Antioch

Two strikingly different figures in Church history, one from the East and one from the West, have both had the name of Ignatius. To many people the better known of the pair is probably the famous Ignatius Loyola, the sixteenth-century soldier-priest and founder of the Jesuit Order, but we are not concerned with him here. The other is Ignatius Theophorus, who was bishop of the metropolitan See of Antioch in Syria in the sub-apostolic age. Although no churchman of that period has a wider renown, there are few of whose lives we know so little. A host of legends grew up about him in later times, but they are unsupported by any real evidence and may be dismissed as quite unhistorical. The truth is that of his origin, birth, and early life we know nothing at all with certainty. It has been surmised from hints in his letters that he was the son of pagan parents, and only converted to Christianity after reaching maturity; this, at least, seems to be the best explanation of his description of himself as 'the last' member of the Syrian Church. A sentence in the fourth chapter of his letter to the Romans has led some commentators to believe that he was a slave, but such an inference probably puts too literal an interpretation on his words. There are also expressions in the epistles suggesting that his youth had been a time of dissipation and self-indulgence, for which like St Augustine he was afterwards to reproach himself bitterly. A tradition which there are no good grounds for disputing credits him with having been a disciple of Apostles; but any further information about his early career is non-existent. Even the significance of his surname Theophorus is an enigma. It was most likely added at baptism, but whether it is to be understood as 'God-borne' or 'God-bearer' (for the word can be translated in either way) is uncertain. The former meaning has been defended by reference to an old legend identifying him with the little child whom Jesus took up in His arms;* but more probably the name should be taken in its active sense, having simply been assumed by Ignatius to express his new character as a Christian – though a later writer prefers the explanation that after the bishop's martyrdom the name of Jesus was found to be inscribed in letters of gold on his heart!

The remainder of his history is scarcely less obscure. He appears to have become bishop of Antioch on the death in A.D. 69 of his predecessor Euodius, who according to Eusebius† had been the first to hold that office after St Peter. But an impenetrable silence lies over the whole forty years of his pastorate. Indeed, if it had not been for the circumstances of his martyrdom, the third bishop of Antioch would doubtless have followed the second into the mists of oblivion; and Ignatius, like Euodius, would be no more to us than another of the unmeaning names that drift among the flotsam of ancient history.

The date usually assigned to his martyrdom is 107, in the reign of the emperor Trajan; but of the reasons for his condemnation, or of the specific charges laid against him, no record survives. At all events, the provincial magistrates at Antioch sentenced him to be thrown to the wild beasts in the arena, and for this purpose dispatched him (probably with other prisoners) in chains to Rome under a guard of ten soldiers. At that time the provinces of the Empire were often required to supply condemned criminals for the Roman circus, and no doubt this accounts for the execution not being carried out at Antioch; though it may also have been thought prudent to avoid the risk of provoking demonstrations of sympathy in the bishop's own city. We can at least be sure that the journey to Rome did not result from an appeal to Caesar by Ignatius himself, as in the case of St Paul; on the contrary, his letters make it clear how earnestly his heart was set on winning the crown of martyrdom, and how genuinely he feared that the 'jealousy of Satan', in the guise of officious friends and well-wishers, might bring about a reprieve and so rob him of the prize.

* *Mark* ix, 36.
† *H.E.* iii, 36 (Penguin edition, p. 145).

The route of the prisoners and their escort took them in a westerly direction by the great trunk road across the continent of Asia Minor. Once past Laodicea, the shortest way to the coast would have been to follow this same road on through Tralles and Magnesia to the sea at Ephesus. But it was the intention of the guards to cross into Europe by the more northerly sea-passage from Troas to Neapolis; and accordingly, after leaving Laodicea, the party quitted the main highway and branched up to the north-west. After passing through the cities of Phila-delphia and Sardis they arrived at Smyrna, where they halted for a while. Ignatius had thus missed the opportunity of seeing the Trallian, Magnesian, and Ephesian churches in the south; but at Smyrna he found to his great pleasure that representatives of all three of them had come up to meet him there, and to bid an affectionate farewell to the martyr-designate. To each of these delegations he gave a letter to take back to their churches at home, and he also sent forward a fourth letter to the Christ-ians at Rome expressing his hopes of meeting them in the near future.

The journey then continued to Troas (whether by land or coasting-vessel we do not know), and while waiting there for the ship to take them across to the opposite coast, Ignatius wrote three more letters. These were addressed to the churches which had recently entertained him when he passed through their cities; one of them went to Philadelphia, another was directed to the congregation at Smyrna, and he also added to this last a personal letter to their bishop Polycarp.

After the departure from Troas there is little more to be said, and for that little we have only tradition to guide us. This records that the final scene took place on the 19th of December in the Flavian amphitheatre, the largest and most famous arena of the ancient world; that the martyr's death there was the work of a moment; and that his bones were afterwards collected by his friends, who obtained permission to carry them back to Antioch and bury them there.

Thus briefly outlined, there seems little that is specially memor-able about such a career. How then are we to account for the remarkable eminence which the Church has since accorded to Ignatius? The threefold answer is found in the character of the man himself, in the theological value of his letters, and in his influence upon subsequent Christian ideas of martyrdom.

As the leader of a great church in an age of storm and stress, Ignatius shows himself to be both wise and fearless, and able to exercise the firmest yet gentlest of discipline. At the same time, we are told that in his personal life he was 'a man in all things like unto the Apostles, and ever vigilant to promote the interests of true piety'; and his letters make this easy to believe. The beauty of holiness shines clearly through their serene and un-questioning faith, their affectionate care for all the churches, and their tender concern for his own. As a revered and sagacious father-in-God the name of Ignatius inspired widespread love and veneration among the Christian communities of his time, and the delegations that flocked to greet him and comfort him on his way to execution are a sufficient proof of the estimation in which he was held.

The Ignatian theology, as it emerges from his writings, embodies three principal ideas: the authority of the clergy, the hatred of heresy and schism, and the glory of martyrdom. Since these were the direct outcome of his experience as bishop of Antioch, some knowledge of the contemporary situation is desirable if we are to understand their development. Antioch, the capital of Syria, was the third of the world's great cities, surpassed only by Rome and Alexandria. Travellers told admiring tales of its magnificence, its wealth, and its luxury; they praised its delicious climate, and the beauty of the mountains and valleys that surrounded it. For three hundred years it had been the royal seat of the kings of Syria; and since then, under the Roman dominion, successive emperors had been increasing its splendour with stately buildings, temples, and works of art. Architects and masons were at work incessantly,* erecting new structures or (for the region was notably liable to earthquakes) restoring the old. Near by, poets and lovers and pleasure-

* Hence, perhaps, Ignatius' elaborate architectural metaphors in *Ephesians* ix.

seekers haunted the shady groves and gardens of Apollo's world-famous sanctuary at Daphne. With all this, however, the moral reputation of the great city was a bad one. Profligacy and vice of all sorts flourished among the mixed multitude of Syrians, Jews, Greeks, and Romans – estimated at half a million in the time of Ignatius – who swarmed and jostled in the elegant avenues and crowded native quarters. Critics even asserted that the licentiousness of its inhabitants made the Queen of the Orient the most degraded of all the Greek cities of the East. In addition, the Antiochenes had an unfavourable name for civic disorders; quarrels and rioting were frequent, and the passions of a hot-tempered, turbulent and excitable populace led to many acts of violence and bloodshed.

This was the city in which, as tradition averred, St Peter had founded the first Gentile church. It was here that his converts had heard for the first time the derisive nickname of 'Christians' shouted after them.* Here money had been collected to relieve the famine-stricken church in Jerusalem, and sent by the hands of Barnabas and Saul.† Here St Paul had exercised his first systematic ministry, and from here he had started on each of his three missionary journeys. Here, only a few years later, the task of Christian leadership in this huge heathen metropolis was placed in the hands of Ignatius.

The immediate problem which confronted him was disunity within the church itself. He found it split into three divergent parties, which we might describe in modern terms as left, right and centre. On the left were the Docetists, whom he saw as the most serious of the dangers threatening the Catholic faith, and against whom he launches his sharpest shafts. On the right were those whose Christianity was still deeply impregnated with the 'old leaven' of Judaism. Midway between the two stood the congregation of faithful believers, with Ignatius as their leader. The paramount need, therefore, as he saw it, was to find some means of creating an undivided church by inducing the dissidents on either side to unite themselves with this central body.

* *Acts* xi, 26.   † *Acts* xi, 30.

67

How was this to be done? The Church of today has means at its disposal for the safeguarding of order and stability; for with a common creed, a canon of Scripture, and a recognized ministry with definite powers, there is little scope for deviation. But Ignatius had not these resources; in his time no common creed was yet in existence, and no Christian writings yet possessed sufficient authority. So, being without credal formulas or written documents to appeal to, he could only fall back on the personal element. If some central authority which should command the respect of all parties was essential, it could be looked for nowhere else but in the body of ordained officials. This is the reason for the repeated and insistent exhortations to obey the bishop and his ministers which occur in all the letters except *Romans*. They have led to the frequently expressed view that the keystone of Ignatian theology is the exaltation of the episcopate; but this is a statement that must be received with caution. It does not justify the imputation to Ignatius of any high sacerdotal doctrine, as is sometimes assumed. The importance he ascribes to the bishop's office is no more and no less than a purely practical measure for imposing unity upon churches which were too often disrupted by internal rivalries and dissensions. Moreover, an examination of the relevant passages shows clearly that it is not the personal authority of the bishop himself that is emphasized, but that of the clerical body as a whole – the threefold ministry of bishop, presbyters, and deacons. Nor, it must be pointed out, does Ignatius take this line because he believes that this episcopal organization is superior to other possible forms of church government – the presbyterial, for instance – but simply because the only alternative to it which he envisages is a wilful and selfish isolation.

This passionate concern for the unity of a divided Church finds its natural complement in the detestation of every form of heresy, which comes out so strongly in the epistles. The most insidious of these, which had sprung up at the very outset of Christianity, and was especially prevalent in Syria and Palestine, was Docetism. It had its origin in an intellectual desire to reconcile religion and philosophy (as we should say, religion and science), and to find a rational explanation for the super-natural. Its adherents, who were influenced by the ideas of Greek and Oriental philosophers about the worthlessness and impurity of everything material, insisted that Christ had not had a real or natural body during His life on earth, but only the appearance (*dokēsis*) of one, and that all His acts and suffer-ings, including the crucifixion and resurrection, were conse-quently illusions. To them, He was a being of such pure spirituality that the attribution to Him of human flesh could not be anything but repugnant. In the earliest form of Docet-ism it had been held that the Godhead descended upon the man Jesus at baptism, endowing him with miraculous powers, and left him again before his death on the cross. (This belief is specially associated with the name of Cerinthus,* who was a contemporary of the Apostle St John and seems to be directly attacked in the Johannine epistles.)† In the time of Ignatius, however, a more thorough-going variant of the heresy was rife, which maintained that the entire human life of Christ from beginning to end had no more than the semblance of reality, His apparent body being only an unsubstantial phantom. It is this false teaching which Ignatius is never tired of denouncing, and which receives its strongest condemnation in his letter to the Smyrnaeans.

Hardly less refractory a thorn in his flesh than Docetism was Judaism. This had always been a source of trouble at Antioch, where the Jewish community was larger than in any other Asian city. It was the same problem that St Paul had encountered for the first time here: the problem which had brought him into collision with St Peter,‡ which had caused the summoning of the first Council of Jerusalem,§ and of which the sounds still echo through his epistle to the Galatians. How far these sec-

---

* The well-known story of St John's hasty exit from the public baths on hearing that Cerinthus was inside is recorded by Eusebius, *H.E.* iii, 28 (Penguin edition, p. 138), and again iv, 14 (ibid., p. 167).

† Cf., e.g., I John i, l, and iv, 3.

‡ *Galatians* ii, 11.

§ *Acts* xv.

taries still retained the practices of orthodox Judaism is not
clear – they had certainly abandoned circumcision – but they
were evidently unwilling to relinquish some of the beliefs and
observances they cherished, and there is no doubt that they
wished to see a larger proportion of Judaism taken into the system of the Church. In a passage in *Philadelphians* Ignatius
takes issue with them over their inability to reconcile the Gospel teachings with their own interpretation of the Old Testament prophets. It has been suggested with much probability
that the members of this group may have been Christianized
Essenes, since their tenets seem to have much in common with
those of the Essene community at Qumran.

But when all is said and done, it was the death rather than
the life of Ignatius that made the deepest impression on the
Church, and led it to see the whole subject of martyrdom in a
fresh light, and to invest it with a new and mystical glory. 'I
am God's wheat', he exulted, 'ground fine by the lions' teeth
to become purest bread for Christ'; and that strange cry of
ecstasy, never heard before, sent a thrill of wonder through the
Christian world. His vision of martyrdom as the crowning
triumph to which a follower of Christ could aspire, his own
passionate desire for it as the supreme prize to be aimed at –
themes which kindle into glowing eloquence in the famous letter to the Romans – had a profound effect on the imagination
of posterity. Many expressions of his became the common cur-
rency of later writers on martyrdom; and as Lightfoot puts it,
'the diction and imagery of martyrologies follow henceforth
in the tracks of Ignatius'.

Note. It should be said that though the opponents of
Ignatius have been represented here as two distinct parties, not
all scholars take this view. Lightfoot, for example, thinks that
there was only one sort of false teaching at Antioch, in which
Docetic and Judaic elements were so closely intermingled as to
form one and the same heresy, called by him Judaeo-Docetism.
Similar opinions are held by the German critics Zahn and Bauer.
The position taken here, on the other hand, is based on the
arguments of Richardson (*The Christianity of Ignatius of*

Antioch) and Virginia Corwin (*St Ignatius and Christianity in Antioch*).

THE EPISTLES

The Ignatian epistles have given rise to a great volume of controversy; and because they contain pronouncements on the very points of Church order which most deeply divide Christian denominations, the arguments both for and against their authenticity have been deployed with much fervour and a wealth of learned ingenuity. Very briefly, the critical position may be summarized as follows. There are in all fifteen epistles attributed to Ignatius, including some letters supposed to be addressed to the Virgin Mary and the Apostle John. By the fifteenth century, however, eight of these had been recognized by all competent judges to be spurious, and this reduced the number to seven. Of these seven there exist two different Greek versions, a longer and a shorter. For many years opinion fluctuated as to which should be accepted; though the views of the disputants were sometimes determined more by their respective attitudes to episcopacy than by purely literary considerations. Bishop Andrews and Richard Hooker, for example, were both in favour of the longer recension; the Puritan Milton, on the other hand, contended hotly for the shorter. In the end the question was decisively settled by the verdict of Archbishop Ussher, whose great work, published in 1644, established beyond reasonable doubt the genuineness of the shorter version.

For the next two centuries after this, the seven Greek epistles in the short form were accepted without serious opposition. But in 1845 a totally new aspect was given to the matter. An official of the British Museum, Dr Cureton, discovered among some manuscripts which had been deposited with him three Ignatian epistles written not in Greek but in the Syriac dialect. They were the letters to the Ephesians, the Romans, and Polycarp. All of these proved to be even briefer than the versions previously known, and Cureton came to the conclusion that they were the only authentic writings of Ignatius. The additional material in the Greek text of them he therefore declared to be interpolated; and all the other four letters he dismissed as forgeries. At once controversy blazed up anew. Were the Greek versions really a later expansion of the original Syriac documents, as Cureton maintained, or were the Syriac manuscripts an abridgement of the earlier Greek? Scholars plunged eagerly into the fray, and the debate went on vigorously until the monumental edition of Lightfoot in 1885 extinguished the flames, completely refuting Cureton's theory and successfully re-establishing the seven epistles in their shorter Greek recension. So the matter rests at the present day.

THE EPISTLE TO THE EPHESIANS

The ancient and wealthy city of Ephesus was the capital of the Roman province of Asia, the richest in the Empire. It was the chief centre of the worship of Artemis (Diana), whose magnificent temple, embellished with the offerings of devotees from every land, was one of the Seven Wonders of the World. Four times the size of the Parthenon, it was the largest temple the Greeks ever built. The Christian church originally planted by St Paul, had had Timothy and the Apostle John for its bishops and was famous as a nursery of saints and martyrs. At this time it was the metropolis of the Asian churches; and though Ignatius had not visited it himself he had a respectful regard for its illustrious reputation. While he and his party were halted at Smyrna, forty miles away, a group of Ephesian representatives headed by their bishop Onesimus had come to greet him there; and he gave them this letter to take back to their congregation. After a tribute to the orderly conduct and doctrinal soundness of the Ephesian Christians, he warns them against the divisions fostered by Docetist teaching, and urges adherence to the bishop and clergy as a safeguard against disunion.

IGNATIUS,
whose other name is Theophorus,

> *To the deservedly happy church at* EPHESUS
> *in Asia; notably blessed with greatness by
> God the Father out of His own fullness;
> marked out since the beginning of time for
> glory unfading and unchanging; and owing
> its unity and its election to the true and un-
> doubted Passion, by the will of the Father and
> Jesus Christ our God.*

*Every good wish to you for perfect joy in
Jesus Christ.*

1. Your visit to me was a godsend. The warm affection your
name inspires is yours by right of nature, as well as by virtue of
your faith and your love for our Saviour Jesus Christ. Taking
God as your pattern and example, you have indeed fulfilled
to perfection the duties of brotherliness, with an ardour kindled
into flame by the Divine Blood. For as soon as you heard that I
was on my way from Syria, as a prisoner for the Name and the
Hope we all share (and trusting through your prayers to be
granted an encounter with the wild beasts at Rome – a boon
that will enable me to become a true disciple), you were all
eagerness to visit me. Thus I have now been able to play the
host, in God's name, to your whole community in the person of
your bishop Onesimus.[1] His endearing kindliness is beyond all
words; I pray you to cherish him in the true spirit of Jesus
Christ, and that every one of you may be the sort of man that
he is. Blessings on Him who gave you the privilege of having
such a bishop, and well indeed do you deserve it.

2. Now, about my fellow-servitor Burrhus, whom God has
made your deacon and endowed with every blessing. Might I
ask you to let him remain here with me?[2] That would do honour both to you and your bishop. Crocus (who also deserves
well of God and you, and whom I welcomed as a shining
example of your love) has been a comfort to me in every way;

75

may the Father of Jesus Christ be as much to him. So also have Onesimus and Burrhus; and Euplus and Fronto too; and in their persons I have had a loving glimpse of you all. May you be a joy to me always, if only I can deserve it.

Now, since Jesus Christ has given such glory to you, it is only right that you should give glory to Him; and this, if sanctification is to be yours in full measure, means uniting in a common act of submission and acknowledging the authority of your bishop and clergy.

3. Not that this is an order I am issuing, as though I were someone of importance. It is true that I am a prisoner for the Name's sake, but I am by no means perfect in Jesus Christ as yet; I am only a beginner in discipleship, and I am speaking to you as fellow-scholars with myself. In fact, it is you who ought really to have given me lessons — lessons in faith and admonishment and patience and toleration. All the same, where you are concerned love will not suffer me to hold my peace; and that is why I venture to recommend an action that reflects the mind of God. For we can have no life apart from Jesus Christ; and as He represents the mind of the Father, so our bishops, even those who are stationed in the remotest parts of the world, represent the mind of Jesus Christ.

4. That is why it is proper for your conduct and your practices to correspond closely with the mind of the bishop. And this, indeed, they are doing; your justly respected clergy, who are a credit to God, are attuned to their bishop like the strings of a harp, and the result is a hymn of praise to Jesus Christ from minds that are in unison, and affections that are in harmony. Pray, then, come and join this choir, every one of you; let there be a whole symphony of minds in concert; take the tone all together from God, and sing aloud to the Father with one voice through Jesus Christ, so that He may hear you and know by your good works that you are indeed members of His Son's Body. A completely united front will help to keep you in constant communion with God.

5. If I myself reached such intimacy with your bishop in a brief space of time — an intimacy that was less of this world

than of the Spirit – how much more fortunate must I count you, who are as inseparably one with him as the Church is with Jesus Christ, and Jesus Christ with the Father; so constituting one single harmonious unity throughout. Let no one be under any illusion; a man who excludes himself from the sanctuary is depriving himself of the bread of God, for if the prayer of one or two individuals has such efficacy, how much more powerful is that of the bishop together with his whole church. Anyone who absents himself from the congregation convicts himself at once of arrogance and becomes self-excommunicate. And since it is written that *God opposes the proud,** let us take care to show no disloyalty to the bishop, so as to be loyal servants of God.

6. The more reserved a bishop is seen to be, the more he ought to be respected. When someone is sent by the master of a house to manage his household for him, it is our duty to give him the same kind of reception as we should give to the sender; and therefore it is clear that we must regard a bishop as the Lord Himself. Onesimus spoke personally in the highest terms of your own correct and godly attitude in this respect; he told me that truth is the guiding principle of your lives, and heresy is so far from gaining a foothold among you that any speaker who goes beyond the simple truth about Jesus Christ is refused a hearing.

7. Nevertheless, there are some people who persistently bandy the Name about with the grossest hypocrisy, besides behaving in a number of other ways that do no credit to God. You must keep away from these men as you would from a pack of savage animals; they are rabid curs who snap at people unawares, and you need to be on your guard against their bites, because they are by no means easy to heal. There is only one Physician –

> Very Flesh, yet Spirit too;
> Uncreated, and yet born;
> God-and-Man in One agreed,
> Very-Life-in-Death indeed,
> Fruit of God and Mary's seed;

* *I Peter* v, 5 (quoting *Proverbs* iii, 34).

At once impassible and torn
By pain and suffering here below:
Jesus Christ, whom as our Lord we know.[3]

8. Let no one, then, mislead you – though being so wholly God's I am sure you have not been misled. So long as there are no deep-seated differences among you, of a kind that could do serious harm, your manner of life is just as God would have it; and my heart goes humbly out to you [4] Ephesians and your ever-famous church. Men who are carnal are no more capable of acting spiritually, nor spiritual men of acting carnally, than deeds of unbelief are possible to the faithful, or deeds of faith to the unbelieving. But with you, even what you do in the flesh is spiritual, for your actions are all done in Jesus Christ.

9. All the same, I did hear of a visit paid to you by certain men from another place, whose teaching was pernicious. However, you refused to allow its dissemination among you, and stopped your ears against the seed they were sowing. Deaf as stones you were: yes, stones for the Father's Temple, stones trimmed ready for God to build with, hoisted up by the derrick of Jesus Christ (the Cross) with the Holy Spirit for a cable; your faith being the winch that draws you to God, up the ramp of love.[5] Again, you are all pilgrims in the same great procession, bearing your God and your shrine and your Christ and your sacred treasures on your shoulders, every one of you arrayed in the festal garments of the commandments of Jesus Christ.[6] And I too have my part in your jubilations, since by virtue of this letter I can count myself one of you, and rejoice with you that your affections are not set upon the things of earthly life, but on God alone.

10. Regarding the rest of mankind, you should pray for them unceasingly, for we can always hope that repentance may enable them to find their way to God. Give them a chance to learn from you, or at all events from the way you act. Meet their animosity with mildness, their high words with humility, and their abuse with your prayers. But stand firm against their errors, and if they grow violent, be gentle instead of wanting to pay them back in their own coin. Let us show by our forbearance

that we are their brothers, and try to imitate the Lord by seeing which of us can put up with the most ill-usage or privation or contempt – so that in this way none of the devil's noxious weeds may take root among you, but you may rest in Jesus Christ in all sanctity and discipline of body and soul.

11. The end of all things is near. From now onwards, then, we must bear ourselves with humility, and tremble at God's patience for fear it should turn into a judgement upon us. Let us either flee from His future wrath, or else embrace His present grace; no matter which, so long as we are found in Jesus Christ with our true life before us. Apart from Him, nothing else should have any value in your eyes; but in Him, even these chains I wear are a collar of spiritual pearls to me,[7] in which I hope to rise again through the help of your intercessions. May there always be a place for me in those intercessions, so that I too may have part and lot among the men of Ephesus – Christians who in the power of Jesus Christ have ever been of the self-same mind as the Apostles themselves.

12. I know well what I am, and what you are to whom I write.[8] I am the condemned; you are the pardoned. I am in peril; you are in security. You are the gateway,[9] through which we are escorted by Death into the presence of God. You are initiates of the same mysteries[10] as our saintly and renowned Paul of blessed memory (may I be found to have walked in his footsteps when I come to God!), who has remembered you in Christ Jesus in every one of his letters.

13. Do your best, then, to meet more often to give thanks and glory to God. When you meet frequently, the powers of Satan are confounded, and in the face of your corporate faith his maleficence crumbles. Nothing can better a state of peaceful accord, from which every trace of spiritual or earthly hostility has been banished.

14. Given a thorough-going faith and love for Jesus Christ, there is nothing in all this that will not be obvious to you; for life begins and ends with those two qualities. Faith is the beginning, and love is the end; and the union of the two together is God. All that makes for a soul's perfection follows in their

train, for nobody who professes faith will commit sin, and nobody who possesses love can feel hatred. As the tree is known by its fruits, so they who claim to belong to Christ are known by their actions; for this work of ours does not consist in just making professions, but in a faith that is both practical and lasting.

15. Indeed, it is better to keep quiet and be, than to make fluent professions and not be. No doubt it is a fine thing to instruct others, but only if the speaker practises what he preaches. One such Teacher there is: He who *spake the word, and it was done;* * and what He achieved even by His silences [11] was well worthy of the Father. A man who has truly mastered the utterances of Jesus will also be able to apprehend His silence, and thus reach full spiritual maturity, so that his own words have the force of actions and his silences the significance of speech. Nothing is hidden from the Lord; even our most secret thoughts are ever present to Him. Whatever we do, then, let it be done as though He Himself were dwelling within us, we being as it were His temples and He within us as their God. For in fact, that is literally the case; and in proportion as we rightly love Him, so it will become clear to our eyes.

16. But let us have no misunderstanding about this, my brothers. No man who is responsible for defiling a household can expect any share in the kingdom of God. Even in the world, defilement of this kind is punishable with death;[12] how much more when a man's subversive doctrines defile the God-given Faith for which Jesus Christ was crucified. Such a wretch in his uncleanness is bound for the unquenchable fire, and so is anyone else who gives him a hearing.

17. The reason for the Lord's acceptance of the precious ointment [13] on His head was to exhale the fragrance of incorruptibility upon His Church. So you must never let yourselves be anointed with the malodorous chrism [14] of the prince of this world's doctrines, or he may snatch you into his own keeping and away from the life that lies before you. (Why can we not all have the good sense to accept that knowledge of God which

* *Psalm* xxxiii, 9.

we have been given, in the person of Jesus Christ? Why must we perish in our folly, ignoring that gracious gift – which in very truth has been sent down to us by the Lord Himself?)

18. As for me, my spirit is now all humble devotion [15] to the Cross: the Cross which so greatly offends the unbelievers, but is salvation and eternal life to us. *Where is your wise man now, or your subtle debater?** Where are the fine words of our so-called intellectuals? Under the Divine dispensation, Jesus Christ our God was conceived by Mary of the seed of David and of the Spirit of God; He was born, and He submitted to baptism, so that by His Passion He might sanctify water.

19. Mary's virginity was hidden from the prince of this world;[16] so was her child-bearing, and so was the death of the Lord. All these three trumpet-tongued secrets [17] were brought to pass in the deep silence of God. How then were they made known to the world? Up in the heavens a star gleamed out, more brilliant than all the rest; no words could describe its lustre, and the strangeness of it left men bewildered. The other stars and the sun and moon gathered round it in chorus, but this star outshone them all. Great was the ensuing perplexity; where could this newcomer have come from, so unlike its fellows? Everywhere magic crumbled away before it;[18] the spells of sorcery were all broken, and superstition received its death-blow. The age-old empire of evil was overthrown, for God was now appearing in human form to bring in a new order, even life without end. Now that which had been perfected in the Divine counsels began its work; and all creation was thrown into a ferment over this plan for the utter destruction of death.

20. I hope to write you a further letter [19] – if, in answer to your prayers, Jesus Christ allows it, and God so wills – in which I will continue this preliminary account for you of God's design for the New Man, Jesus Christ. It is a design which provides for faith in Him and love for Him, and comprehends His Passion and His Resurrection. I will certainly do this if the Lord

* *I Cor.* i, 20.

reveals to me that you are all, man by man and name by name, attending your meetings in a state of grace, united in faith and in Jesus Christ (who is the seed of David according to the flesh, and is the Son of Man and Son of God), and are ready now to obey your bishop and clergy with undivided minds and to share in the one common breaking of bread – the medicine of immortality, and the sovereign remedy by which we escape death and live in Jesus Christ for evermore.

21. I am offering my life on your behalf, and also for those whom you sent for the honour of God here to Smyrna, where I am writing this letter. It carries my gratitude to God, as well as my love to Polycarp and yourselves. Remember me, as Jesus Christ remembers you. Pray for the church in Syria, from which they are bringing me in chains to Rome. I was the last and least of the faithful there, and yet I have been deemed worthy to set forward the honour of God.

Farewell to you, in God the Father and in Jesus Christ, who is our common Hope.

NOTES

1. It is unlikely that he was (as some have thought) the slave mentioned in St Paul's *Epistle to Philemon*, who would scarcely be still living at this time.

2. This request was granted, for when Ignatius left Smyrna the Smyrnaeans joined with the Ephesians in finding the money for Burrhus to go on with him as far as Troas, as a companion and secretary. Most probably, therefore, it was Burrhus who brought back from Troas the letters written there to Philadelphia, Smyrna, and Polycarp.

3. The rhythmical nature of this passage has tempted some commentators to see it as an excerpt from an early Christian hymn – a temptation which I have not resisted.

4. Literally 'I am your off-scouring, dregs, refuse:' a word used of the lowest of criminals, whose blood was shed as an offering to avert the anger of the gods. Later, however, it becomes an epistolary formality meaning little more than 'your humble servant'.

5. For the elaborate architectural imagery of this passage, see the footnote on p. 66.

6. Here the metaphor changes abruptly, and is now taken from the religious ceremonies of the heathen. These were a familiar spectacle at Ephesus, where processions of worshippers in festal garments paraded the streets carrying sacred emblems, statues of the gods, model shrines, and precious objects from the famous temple of Artemis.

7. 'He is proud of this decoration, with which his Sovereign has invested him' (Lightfoot). The curious pleasure which Ignatius takes in his chains recurs at nearly every mention of them in his letters.

8. Here Ignatius breaks off to insert a brief apology for presuming, as a mere condemned criminal, to exhort the illustrious church of Ephesus.

9. Literally, an entrance, passage, or approach-route. Ephesus, at the end of the great highway across Asia Minor, must have been a staging-point for many Christian martyrs on their way to execution at Rome.

10. St Paul had lived for a long time among the Ephesians (*Acts* xix, 10 and xx, 31). In his epistle to them he several times refers to the Gospel teachings as 'mysteries'; and elsewhere (*Philippians* iv, 12) he describes himself as 'initiated'.

11. Here Ignatius is probably thinking not so much of the silence of passivity (e.g. Christ's repeated refusals to allow publication of His miracles, His silence when questioned by the High Priest and Pilate, and so forth) as of the dynamic effects of His simply being what He was. See note 16 below.

12. Alluding to the punishment of adulterers. Ignatius's language about the 'defilement' of the Faith by the false teachers is perhaps not wholly figurative, since many of the principal heresies excused sexual immorality on the ground that all material things (including the flesh) were worthless and unimportant.

13. The incident is recorded in *Matthew* xxvi, 7.

14. The ointment used in baptism. Ignatius seems to have the rite in mind here, as he refers to its other element (water) in the next section.

15. Literally 'offscouring', the word used before in ch. 8, where see note 4.

16. Few statements of Ignatius are more often quoted by later patristic writers than this. The notion that the devil was completely

hoodwinked by the secrecy of the Incarnation became a favourite in early theology. This idea of God's 'silence', mentioned in the next sentence, has a prominent place in Ignatian thought. The word stands for the unrevealed depths of His Being, the vast hidden reserves of power, which are for ever beyond man's knowledge. It seems to be similarly used in reference to Jesus (ch. 15) and even to contemporary bishops (ch. 6; also *Philadelphians* i).

17. Literally 'these mysteries of a loud shout'; a deliberately paradoxical expression. They were prepared in the silence of God, in order to be proclaimed aloud to the world.

18. It was commonly believed that magic, which played a large part in the pagan religions, was destroyed by the Incarnation, and that the visit of the Magi typified its capitulation.

19. Nothing is known of any such letter. Perhaps there was no opportunity of composing it during the remaining stages of his journey to execution.

*

THE EPISTLE TO THE
MAGNESIANS

*

Magnesia-on-the-Maeander (so called to distinguish it from its neighbour Magnesia-under-Sipylus and from a third Magnesia in Thessaly) was fifteen miles from Ephesus, and its church, like that of the Ephesians, had sent a delegation to meet Ignatius at Smyrna, led by their bishop Damas. Writing in acknowledgement of this visit, Ignatius cautions them against presuming upon Damas's youth and inexperience, and goes on to stress the need for ensuring unity by a complete obedience to the bishop's authority. In this letter there is a more specific denunciation of the 'old leaven' of Judaistic doctrines and observances than in his other epistles.

From IGNATIUS,
whose other name is Theophorus,

> *To the church at* MAGNESIA-ON-THE-
> MAEANDER, *blessed by the grace of God
> the Father in Christ Jesus our Saviour, in
> whom I send these greetings.*

*All happiness to you, in God the
Father and in Jesus Christ.*

1. When I heard of the disciplined way of life your Christian love has taught you, it gave me so much pleasure that I decided to address a few words to you in the faith of Jesus Christ. As I go about in these chains, invested with a title worthy of a god, I sing songs of praise to the churches;[1] and I pray for their corporate as well as their spiritual unity – for both of these are the gifts of Jesus Christ, our never-failing Life. May they be one in their faith, and one in the love which transcends all other virtues; but chiefest of all may they be one with Jesus and the Father, since it is only by enduring in Him all the prince of this world's indignities, yet still eluding his clutches, that we can come to the presence of God.

2. It was my privilege to have a glimpse of you in the persons of your saintly bishop Damas and his two clergy, the worthy Bassus and Apollonius, as well as my fellow-servitor Zotion the deacon. I should be happy in that man's company; he is as deferential to his bishop as he is to the grace of God, and to his clergy as to the law of Jesus Christ.

3. For your part, the becoming thing for you to do is to take no advantage of your bishop's lack of years, but to show him every possible respect, having regard to the power God has conferred on him. My information is that the sacred clergy themselves never think of presuming on the apparent precocity of his rank; they give precedence to him as a sagacious man of God – or rather, not so much to him as to the Father of Him who is the Bishop of us all, Jesus Christ. So for the honour of Him who loved us, propriety requires an obedience from you that is more

than mere lip-service. It is not a question of imposing upon a particular bishop who is there before your eyes, but upon One who is unseen; and in such a case it is not flesh and blood we have to reckon with, but God, who is aware of all our secrets.

4. What it comes to is that we ought not just to have the name of Christians, but to be so in reality; not like some persons who will address a man as bishop, but in practice take no notice of him. I do not see how people of that kind can be acting in good conscience, seeing that the meetings they hold can have no sort of valid authority.[2]

5. All things must come to an end, and there are two alternatives before us. They are life and death; and every one of us will have to go to his own particular place. There are two different coinages, so to speak, in circulation, God's and the world's, each with its own distinctive marking. Unbelievers carry the stamp of the world; while the faithful in love bear the stamp of God the Father, through Jesus Christ. Unless we are ready and willing to die in conformity with His Passion, His life is not in us.

6. And now, since I have already seen with the eyes of faith and embraced your whole congregation, in the persons of the men I named, let me urge on you the need for godly unanimity in everything you do. Let the bishop preside in the place of God, and his clergy in place of the Apostolic conclave,[3] and let my special friends the deacons be entrusted with the service of Jesus Christ, who was with the Father from all eternity and in these last days has been made manifest. Everyone should observe the closest conformity with God; you must show every consideration for one another, never letting your attitude to a neighbour be affected by your human feelings, but simply loving each other consistently in the spirit of Jesus Christ. Allow nothing whatever to exist among you that could give rise to any divisions; maintain absolute unity with your bishop and leaders, as an example to others and a lesson in the avoidance of corruption.

7. In the same way as the Lord was wholly one with the Father, and never acted independently of Him, either in person or through the Apostles, so you yourselves must never act independently of your bishop and clergy. On no account persuade

yourselves that it is right and proper to follow your own private judgement; have a single service of prayer which everybody attends; one united supplication, one mind, one hope, in love and innocent joyfulness. All of you together, as though you were approaching the only existing temple of God and the only altar, speed to the one and only Jesus Christ – who came down from the one and only Father, is eternally with that One, and to that One is now returned.

8. Never allow yourselves to be led astray by the teachings and the time-worn fables of another people.[4] Nothing of any use can be got from them. If we are still living in the practice of Judaism, it is an admission that we have failed to receive the gift of grace. Even the lives of their divinely inspired prophets were instinct with Jesus Christ. Indeed, the only reason they were persecuted is because they were inspired by His grace, so that they might convince future unbelievers of the existence of one sole God, who has revealed Himself in His Son Jesus Christ, Word of His own from silence proceeding, who in all that He was and did gladdened the heart of the One who sent Him.

9. We have seen how former adherents of the ancient customs have since attained to a new hope; so that they have given up keeping the sabbath, and now order their lives by the Lord's Day instead (the Day when life first dawned for us, thanks to Him and His death. That death, though some deny it,[5] is the very mystery which has moved us to become believers, and endure tribulation to prove ourselves pupils of Jesus Christ, our sole Teacher). In view of this, how can it be possible for us to give Him no place in our lives,[6] when even the prophets of old were themselves pupils of His in spirit, and looked forward to Him as their Teacher? Indeed, that was the very reason why He, whom they were rightly awaiting, came to visit them, and raised them from the dead.[7]

10. Do not let us be blind to His goodness, then. If He were ever to imitate the way we ourselves behave, it would be all over with us. Now that we have become pupils of His, let us learn to live like Christians. To profess any other name but that is to be lost to God; so lay aside the old good-for-nothing leaven, now

grown stale and sour, and change to the new, which is Jesus
Christ. Have yourselves salted in Him, and then there will be no
scent of corruption about any of you – for it is by your odour
that you will be proved. To profess Jesus Christ while continuing
to follow Jewish customs is an absurdity. The Christian faith
does not look to Judaism, but Judaism looks to Christianity,[8] in
which every other race and tongue that confesses a belief in God
has now been comprehended.

11. In pointing these things out to you, my brothers, it is not
that I know of any of you being actually affected in this way; it
is simply that I am anxious, in all humility, to warn you in
good time of the pitfalls of this shallow teaching. I want you to
be unshakably convinced of the Birth, the Passion, and the
Resurrection which were the true and indisputable experiences
of Jesus Christ, our Hope, in the days of Pontius Pilate's gov-
ernorship. God grant that none of you may ever be turned aside
from that Hope.

12. My desire is to enjoy every happiness in you – that is, if
I am worthy of it; for even though I have chains to wear and
you have none, I am still unfit to bear comparison with any one
of you. For you, as I know so well, are wholly free from pride,
having Jesus Christ within you; and I am aware that any praise
from me only makes you more distrustful of yourselves – even
as, in the words of Scripture, *the righteous man is his own
accuser.**

13. Do your utmost to stand firm in the precepts of the Lord
and the Apostles, so that everything you do, worldly or spiritual, may go prosperously from beginning to end in faith and
love, in the Son and the Father and the Spirit, together with
your most reverend bishop and that beautifully-woven spiritual
chaplet, your clergy and godly minded deacons. Be as submissive to the bishop and to one another as Jesus Christ was to His
Father, and as the Apostles were to Christ and the Father; so
that there may be complete unity, in the flesh as well as in the
spirit.

14. Knowing how amply filled with God you are, I have been

* The Septuagint's rendering of *Proverbs* xviii, 17.

brief in these exhortations. Remember me in your prayers, so that I may win my way to God; and remember the church in Syria too, of which I am an unworthy member. I beg for your united prayers and love in God, so that our Syrian church may be refreshed with a sprinkling of dew from yours.

15. The representatives of Ephesus send greetings to you from Smyrna here, where I am writing this. Like yourselves,[9] they are here for the glory of God, and they have been a comfort to me in every way. So too has Polycarp, the Smyrnaean bishop. The other churches add their own greetings as well, for the honour of Jesus Christ.

Farewell. See that there is a godly unity among you, and a spirit that is above all divisions; for this is Jesus Christ.

NOTES

1. The picture is that of a reveller in his holiday finery, singing for joy. For Ignatius's innocent pride in his chains see *Ephesians* xi and note.

2. The services of the dissident faction, being held without the presence or sanction of the bishop, were considered irregular and invalid.

3. In the services of the early Church the bishop occupied a seat on a dais at the centre of a semi-circle of his clergy (an arrangement copied from the position of judge and assessors in the law-courts). This suggests a comparison with the Apostles on their twelve thrones around the Throne of God; the earthly hierarchy being thus a type of the heavenly. The same image recurs in *Trallians* 3.

4. The reference is to certain heretical forms of Christianity which combined Judaistic with Docetic elements, and are repeatedly denounced by the New Testament writers (eg. *Colossians* ii, 18–23, *Titus* iii, 9, etc). The 'time-worn fables' are the popular Jewish legends of cosmogony, angelology, devils, and so forth.

5. i.e. the Docetists, who denied the reality of the Passion.

6. Either by the Docetic rejection of His death and resurrection, through which we are united to Him, or by the Judaistic reliance on forms and rules instead of on His grace.

7. It was believed that when Christ descended into Hades He preached the Gospel to the saints of the Old Testament there, and raised them up to life in heaven. This, which is referred to in *I Peter* iii, 19 and iv, 6, was known in the Middle Ages as the Harrowing of Hell.

8. Christianity. This is the earliest known appearance of this noun in literature. Ignatius uses it again in *Romans* 3 and *Philadelphians* 6.

9. The Magnesians are assumed to be present in the persons of their representatives.

*

THE EPISTLE TO THE TRALLIANS

*

Tralles, a busy and affluent city, lay seventeen miles to the eastward of Magnesia, on the highroad from Laodicea to Ephesus. The Trallian church, like its neighbours, had heard that Ignatius would be passing through Smyrna, and its grave and gentle bishop Polybius had gone there to greet him. Writing in response, Ignatius opens with his customary recommendation of obedience to clerical authority; and then, excusing himself from a discussion of such loftier themes as had perhaps been expected of him, concentrates on the more urgent danger from the adherents of Docetism, who here receive their most forcible condemnation.

From IGNATIUS,
whose other name is Theophorus,

> To the holy church at TRALLES *in Asia;*
> *beloved of God the Father of Jesus Christ,*
> *elect and godly, endowed with peace of body*
> *and soul by the Passion of Jesus Christ, who*
> *through our rising again to Him is our Hope.*

In apostolic fashion, I send the church my
greeting in all the fullness of God, and wish
her every happiness.

1. They tell me that your character is beyond all praise, and never falters in its endurance; and that this is not just a habit you have acquired, but your own natural disposition. I had that from your bishop Polybius, when the will of God and Jesus Christ brought him here to me in Smyrna. He was so full of joy with me in my bonds in Christ Jesus, that in him I had a vision of your whole congregation; and when I received from his hands the token of your goodwill [1] under God for me, I gave glory for finding that you were as truly imitators of God as I had been assured.

2. Your obedience to your bishop, as though he were Jesus Christ, shows me plainly enough that yours is no worldly manner of life, but that of Jesus Christ Himself, who gave His life for us that faith in His death might save you from death. At the same time, however, essential as it is that you should never act independently of the bishop – as evidently you do not – you must also be no less submissive to your clergy, and regard them as apostles of Jesus Christ our Hope, in whom we shall one day be found, if our lives are lived in Him. The deacons too, who serve the mysteries of Jesus Christ, must be men universally approved in every way; since they are not mere dispensers of meat and drink, but servants of the church of God, and therefore under obligation to guard themselves against any slur or imputation as strictly as they would against fire itself.

3. Equally, it is for the rest of you to hold the deacons in as

great respect as Jesus Christ; just as you should also look on the bishop as a type of the Father, and the clergy as the Apostolic circle[2] forming His council; for without these three orders no church has any right to the name. I am sure these are your own feelings too, for I have had with me, and still have, an example of your affection in the person of your bishop himself, whose grave demeanour is a notable lesson in itself, and whose very gentleness is power. I cannot doubt that even the heathen have a respect for him. I am measuring my words here, out of love for you, for I could well write more forcibly on his behalf, if it were not that as a condemned prisoner I have not thought myself entitled to use the peremptory tone of an Apostle.

4. God has certainly filled my head with a great many thoughts; but I am careful of my own limitations, for fear boasting should be the downfall of me. The sentiments I ought rather to be feeling are apprehension, and a disregard of all those who seek to flatter me.[3] The words of those people are real scourges to me; for much as I yearn for martyrdom, I am not at all sure of being found worthy of it. So many of them fail to perceive Satan's jealousy,[4] which thus becomes all the more formidable an adversary to me. Consequently I have great need of that humility which is the prince of this world's undoing.

5. So, though I could, no doubt, write to you on high and heavenly topics, I fear it might only be to your detriment, seeing that you are still in your infancy. Forgive me, then; for they might well be beyond your power to assimilate, and would only stick in your throats. Even I myself, for all my chains and for all my ability to comprehend celestial secrets and angelic hierarchies and the dispositions of the heavenly powers, and much else both seen and unseen, am not yet on that account a real disciple. For there is much that we must still fall short of, if we are not to fall short of God.

6. And so I entreat you (not I, though, but the love of Jesus Christ) not to nourish yourselves on anything but Christian fare, and have no truck with the alien herbs of heresy. There are men who in the very act of assuring you of their good faith will mingle poison with Jesus Christ; which is like offering a lethal

drug in a cup of honeyed wine, so that the unwitting victim blissfully accepts his own destruction with a fatal relish.

7. Guard yourselves carefully against men of that sort. You will be safe enough so long as you do not let pride go to your head and break away from Jesus Christ and your bishop and the Apostolic institutions.[5] To be inside the sanctuary[6] is to be clean; to be outside it, unclean. In other words, nobody's conscience can be clean if he is acting without the authority of his bishop, clergy, and deacons.

8. Not that I suspect anything of the kind among you; I am only trying to protect you in good time, because you are dear to my heart and I can foresee the devil's snares ahead. So let submission and unselfishness be your weapons against them; take a fresh grip on your faith (the very flesh of the Lord)[7] and your love (the life-blood of Jesus Christ), for there must not be any ill-feeling between neighbours. You must give the heathen no loophole, for fear the devout majority are brought into disrepute for the thoughtlessness of a few; for *woe to him who makes anyone blaspheme my Name without a cause.**

9.[8] Close your ears, then, if anyone preaches to you without speaking of Jesus Christ. Christ was of David's line. He was the son of Mary; He was verily and indeed born, and ate and drank; He was verily persecuted in the days of Pontius Pilate, and verily and indeed crucified, and gave up the ghost in the sight of all heaven and earth and the powers of the nether world. He was also verily raised up again from the dead, for His Father raised him; and in Jesus Christ will His Father similarly raise us who believe in Him, since apart from Him there is no true life for us.

10. It is asserted by some who deny God – in other words, who have no faith – that His sufferings were not genuine (though in fact it is themselves in whom there is nothing genuine). If this is so, then why am I now a prisoner? Why am I praying for a combat with the lions? For in that case, I am giving away my life for nothing; and all the things I have ever said about the Lord are untruths.

* Apparently a confused recollection of *Isaiah* lii, 5.

11. Flee for your very life from these men; they are poisonous growths with a deadly fruit, and one taste of it is speedily fatal. They are none of the Father's planting; if they were, they could at once be known for true branches of the Cross, and there would be no corruption in their fruit. It is by the Cross that through His Passion He calls you, who are parts of His own Body, to Himself. A Head cannot come into being alone, without any limbs; for the promise that we have from God is the promise of unity, which is the essence of Himself.

12. The other churches of God which are here with me join in this message of greetings from Smyrna. (They have been every sort of natural and spiritual solace to me.) These chains, which I wear for Jesus Christ's sake in my constant entreaty to reach the presence of God, utter their own appeal to you to continue in unity and prayerfulness with one another. For it is the duty of everyone, and most particularly of the clergy, to see that the bishop enjoys peace of mind, for the honour of the Father and Jesus Christ and His Apostles, I beg you, as you love me, give heed to what I say, so that I may not rise up in evidence against you one day with this letter. And pray for me as well; for in God's mercy I need your love, if I am ever to be granted the fate I long for, and am not to be rejected.

13. Smyrna and Ephesus send you their love and greetings. Remember my Syrian church in your prayers (though I do not deserve to be called a member of it, since I am the last and least of them all).

Farewell now in Jesus Christ. Defer to your bishop as you would to the Divine Law, and likewise to your clergy. Love one another, all of you, with a heart above all divisions. My spirit offers itself on your behalf, not only now but also when I shall stand in the presence of God. Whether that will happen is still in hazard; but the Father may be trusted in Jesus Christ to grant my supplications and yours. May you be found faultless in Him.

NOTES

1. This goodwill, it seems, had taken the practical form of a present of some kind.

2. For the origin of this comparison see note 3 on *Magnesians* 6. (That Ignatius has inadvertently given the deacons a higher position than the presbyters shows the danger of carrying a figure too far.)

3. He has in mind the favourable reports made of him by well-meaning friends, in the hope of persuading the authorities to reconsider his condemnation.

4. Satan's jealousy. Though the name does not appear in the text, it is quite clear whose 'jealousy' is intended. Ignatius means that the good offices of his friends are in reality prompted by the devil, who envies the martyr his crown.

5. Specifically, the institution of episcopacy, traditionally established in Asia Minor by the Apostle St John.

6. Literally, the place of sacrifice, signifying here the assembled congregation of ministers and people.

7. 'Faith is the *flesh*, the *substance* of the Christian life; love is the *blood*, the *energy* coursing through its veins and arteries' (Lightfoot).

8. Sections 9, 10, and 11 sums up the message of the epistle, in a final re-assertion of the reality of Christ's humanity and a warning against the Docetists who denied it.

THE EPISTLE TO THE
ROMANS

This letter, the most personal and moving of all the epistles, is in striking contrast with the other six. For once, the familiar topics are all laid aside; there are no more warnings against heresy (on the contrary, the Romans are declared to be 'purified from every alien and discolouring stain'), no demands for obedience to the bishop (it is the only letter which never even mentions that official), and no references to church unity. Instead, Ignatius is wholly occupied here with the subject of his own approaching martyrdom. He shows himself longing for his fate with a lover's passion; he implores the Romans on no account to deprive him of his crown by any officious attempts to obtain a pardon for him; and he exalts the glories of the martyr's death with a lyrical rapture. In after ages this became the most popular and widely quoted of all the Ignatian writings; its influence on persecuted Christians everywhere was enormous, and it took permanent rank as a kind of 'martyrs' manual'.

From IGNATIUS,
whose other name is Theophorus,

> *To her who has found mercy in the greatness of the All-Highest Father, and Jesus Christ His only Son; to the church beloved and enlightened in her love to our God Jesus Christ by the will of Him who wills all things; to the church holding chief place in the territories of the district of* ROME[1] *— worthy of God, worthy of honour, blessing, praise, and success; worthy too in holiness, foremost in love, observing the law of Christ, and bearing the Father's Name.*

Greeting, in the Name of Jesus Christ the Father's Son. All perfect happiness in Jesus Christ our God, to you who are bodily and spiritually at one with all His commandments, whole-heartedly filled with the grace of God, and purified[2] from every alien and discolouring stain.

1. My prayers that I might live to see your devoted community face to face have been answered; indeed, I have been granted more than I asked for, since I can now hope to greet you in the very chains[3] of a prisoner of Jesus Christ, if His will permits me to reach my journey's end. So far, things have made an admirable beginning; and all now depends on whether I can reach the goal and secure my inheritance without hindrance. But what fills me with fear is your own kindly feeling for me, and the disservice it may do me.[4] What you are bent on doing will certainly present no difficulties for yourselves, but for me it is going to be very hard to get to God unless you spare me your intervention.

2. It is not men that I want you to gratify,[5] but God, just as you habitually do. I shall never have a better chance than this of getting to God; and you on your part will never have a finer piece of work to your credit, if only you will keep your lips sealed. For by staying silent and letting me alone, you can turn

me into an intelligible utterance of God;[6] but if your affections are only concerned with my poor human life, then I become a mere meaningless cry once more. This favour only I beg of you: suffer me to be a libation poured out to God,[7] while there is still an altar ready for me. Then you may form a loving choir around it and sing hymns of praise in Jesus Christ to the Father, for permitting Syria's bishop, summoned from the realms of the morning, to have reached the land of the setting sun.[8] How good it is to be sinking down below the world's horizon towards God, to rise again later into the dawn of His presence!

3. It was never your way to grudge anyone his success. You have been a source of instruction to others;[9] all I want is for the principles which you expound by your teaching to hold good now. The only petition I would have you put forward on my behalf is that I may be given sufficient inward and outward strength to be as resolute in will as in words, and a Christian in reality instead of only in repute (though once I have the reality, I can have the repute too, and be held loyal and true even when the world can see me no longer. For good does not reside in what our eyes can see; the fact that Jesus Christ is now within the Father is why we perceive Him so much the more clearly. For the work we have to do is no affair of persuasive speaking; Christianity lies in achieving greatness in the face of a world's hatred.

4. For my part, I am writing to all the churches and assuring them that I am truly in earnest about dying for God – if only you yourselves put no obstacles in the way. I must implore you to do me no such untimely kindness; pray leave me to be a meal for the beasts, for it is they who can provide my way to God. I am His wheat, ground fine by the lions' teeth to be made purest bread [10] for Christ. Better still, incite the creatures to become a sepulchre for me; let them not leave the smallest scrap of my flesh, so that I need not be a burden to anyone after I fall asleep. When there is no trace of my body left for the world to see, then I shall truly be Jesus Christ's disciple. So intercede with Him for me, that by their instrumentality I may be made a sacrifice to God. However, I am not issuing orders to you, as though I were

a Peter or a Paul.[11] They were Apostles, and I am a condemned criminal. They were free men, and I am still a slave [12] (though if I suffer, Jesus Christ will give me my liberty, and in Him I shall rise again as a free man). For the present, these chains are schooling me to have done with earthly desires.

5. All the same, I have already been finding myself in conflict with beasts of prey by land and by sea,[13] by night and by day, the whole way from Syria to Rome; chained as I am to half-a-score of savage leopards [14] (in other words, a detachment of soldiers), who only grow more insolent the more gratuities they are given. Still, their ill-usage does at least enable me to make some progress in discipleship; though that is not to say that my sins are yet wholly absolved. How I look forward to the real lions that have been got ready for me! All I pray is that I may find them swift. I am going to make overtures to them, so that, unlike some other wretches whom they have been too spiritless to touch, they may devour me with all speed. And if they are still reluctant, I shall use force to them. You must forgive me, but I do know what is best for myself. This is the first stage of my discipleship; and no power, visible or invisible, must grudge me my coming to Jesus Christ. Fire, cross, beast-fighting, hacking and quartering, splintering of bone and mangling of limb, even the pulverizing of my entire body – let every horrid and diabolical torment come upon me, provided only that I can win my way to Jesus Christ!

6. All the ends of the earth, all the kingdoms of the world would be of no profit to me; so far as I am concerned, to die in Jesus Christ is better than to be monarch of earth's widest bounds. He who died for us is all that I seek; He who rose again for us is my whole desire. The pangs of birth are upon me; have patience with me, my brothers, and do not shut me out from life, do not wish me to be stillborn. Here is one who only longs to be God's; do not make a present of him to the world again, or delude him with the things of earth. Suffer me to attain to light, light pure and undefiled; for only when I am come thither shall I be truly a man. Leave me to imitate the Passion of my God. If any of you has God within himself, let that man understand

my longings, and feel for me, because he will know the forces by which I am constrained.

7. It is the hope of this world's prince to get hold of me and undermine my resolve, set as it is upon God. Pray let none of you lend him any assistance, but take my part instead, for it is the part of God. Do not have Jesus Christ on your lips, and the world in your heart; do not cherish thoughts of grudging me my fate. Even if I were to come and implore you in person, do not yield to my pleading; keep your compliance for this written entreaty instead. Here and now, as I write in the fullness of life, I am yearning for death with all the passion of a lover. Earthly longings have been crucified; in me there is left no spark of desire for mundane things, but only a murmur of living water that whispers within me, 'Come to the Father'. There is no pleasure for me in any meats that perish, or in the delights of this life; I am fain for the bread of God, even the flesh of Jesus Christ, who is the seed of David; and for my drink I crave that Blood of His which is love imperishable.

8. I want no more of what men call life. And my want can come true, if it is your desire. Pray, then, let it be your desire; so that in your turn you also may be desired.[15] Not to write at more length, I appeal to you to believe me. Jesus Christ will make it clear to you that I am speaking the truth; he is a faithful mouthpiece, by which the Father's words of truth find utterance. Intercede for me, then, that I may have my wish; for I am not writing now as a mere man, but I am voicing the mind of God. My suffering will be a proof of your goodwill; my rejection, a proof of your disfavour.

9. Remember the church of Syria in your prayers; it has God for its pastor now, in place of myself, and Jesus Christ alone will have the oversight of it – He, and your own love. As for me, I feel shame to be styled one of its members; I have no right at all to the name, for I was the very last of them all, an embryo born untimely[16] (though if I ever manage to reach the presence of God, by His mercy I shall be somebody then).

I greet you in spirit; and the churches who have been my hosts in the name of Jesus Christ also send you their love. (It was no common wayfarer's welcome I have had from them, for even churches that were not naturally on my route at all came and escorted me from one city to the next.)

10. This letter comes to you from Smyrna, by the hands of our praiseworthy men of Ephesus. Crocus, specially dear to me, is here too, and a number of others besides. I believe you have already been told of certain persons who went on ahead of me from Syria to Rome, for the glory of God. Tell them that I am not far away now. One and all, they have deserved well of God and of you; and it is only right for you to do what you can to set their minds at rest.

As I write this, it is the twenty-fourth of August. Farewell now until the end, and wait with patience for Jesus Christ.

NOTES

1. This curious phraseology seems to indicate a Christian organization under which the Roman church possessed a religious and administrative predominance among the other churches of the region.

2. Literally 'filtered out': the technical word which is used in St Matthew's Gospel for 'straining out' a gnat. Ignatius employs the same metaphor again in *Philadelphians* 3.

3. He hopes not only to visit them, but to visit them adorned with the chains of a prisoner for Jesus Christ. The fancy that his fetters are an honourable decoration recurs in the letters to the Ephesians (*Eph.* 3 and 11) and Magnesians (*Mag.* 1).

4. He is afraid that influential friends in Rome may succeed in obtaining a pardon for him, and so frustrate his hopes of martyrdom.

5. By seconding the efforts of those who were trying to save him.

6. An intelligible utterance of God: 'an expression testifying to the Gospel; a manifestation of the Divine purpose' (Lightfoot).

7. St Paul twice applies this same description to himself (*Philippians* ii, 17 and *II Timothy* iv, 6) in connexion with the contests in the arena. The 'altar ready' for the libation is the Flavian amphitheatre in which Ignatius was to die.

8. Italy, the 'Far West' to a bishop from Syria.

9. St Peter, St Paul, and many another martyr of the Roman church

had gone bravely to their deaths in the persecutions under Nero and Domitian.

10. Only bread of the finest quality, as a symbol of purity, was used in sacrificial offerings.

11. Both of whom had been at Rome, and spoken with apostolic authority to the Roman church.

12. This has led some commentators to think that Ignatius had been, or perhaps still was, an actual slave. It may only refer, however, to his present helpless condition.

13. If this is meant literally, we must assume that the first stage of his journey had been made by ship from Seleucia (the port of Antioch) to Attalia, in Pamphylia. From there the party could make their way overland to Laodicea.

14. This is the earliest known occurrence of the word in literature. Since leopards were well known in Syria (whence they were sometimes brought for exhibition at Rome) the comparison would come naturally to Ignatius.

15. i.e., by God.

16. St Paul, too, describes himself in the same way (*I Cor.* xv, 8). Here, as there, the image suggests both a sudden conversion to Christianity, and a slow and feeble growth.

THE EPISTLE TO THE PHILADELPHIANS

This is the first of the three letters written by Ignatius after his arrival at Troas. Recently, on his way thither from Smyrna, he had passed through Philadelphia and met the members of its church; and affectionate memories of the visit are still fresh in his mind as he writes. Since many of the local Christians were converts from the large Jewish community in Philadelphia (which the Book of Revelation calls 'the synagogue of Satan'), disturbing signs of Judaism were showing themselves in the church. The main purpose of the letter is to controvert these errors; and here, as elsewhere, Ignatius urges unity and obedience to the bishop as the most efficacious remedy.

During his stay at Troas, news had reached him that the persecution of Christians in his own city of Antioch had now died down. He therefore suggests that the Philadelphians should follow the example of other churches and send one of their deacons to Antioch with a message of congratulation. The length of such a journey and its arduous nature make this a striking instance of the brotherly feelings which linked the Christian churches of the period.

From IGNATIUS,
whose other name is Theophorus,

> To the church of God the Father and the Lord Jesus Christ at PHILADELPHIA *in Asia; mercifully settled in all godly concord; steadfastly rejoicing in the passion and resurrection of our Lord; and in the fullness of His mercy, holding sure and certain conviction of the same.*

I send you my greetings in the Blood of Jesus Christ, wherein is joy eternal and unfailing; all the more so when men are at one with their bishop – and with their clergy and deacons too, whose appointment with him is approved by Jesus Christ, and confirmed and ratified, according to His will, by His Holy Spirit.

1. Your bishop's office, which exists for the good of the whole community, was never obtained by his own efforts, as I know very well, nor by any other mere human agency, still less in any spirit of self-glorification; but it was conferred upon him by the love of God the Father and the Lord Jesus Christ. I was deeply impressed by his self-effacing nature; reserve in him is more effectual than any volubility in others. He is as utterly in tune with the Divine precepts as a harp with its own strings; and I call down blessings in my heart on a mind so turned towards God, for I can recognize its perfections, and the passionless serenity of a life that is lived in such heavenly mildness.

2. As children of the light of truth, therefore, see that you hold aloof from all disunion and misguided teaching; and where your bishop is, there follow him like sheep. There are plausible wolves in plenty seeking to entrap the runners in God's race with their perilous allurements; but so long as there is solidarity among you, they will find no room for themselves.

3. Have nothing to do with such poisonous weeds; they are none of the Father's planting, nor have they Jesus Christ for their husbandman. (I am not saying, though, that I found you in any sort of actual division; it was only the filtering out of a few dregs.) Every man who belongs to God and Jesus Christ stands by his bishop. As for the rest, if they repent and come back into the unity of the church, they too shall belong to God, and so bring their lives into conformity with Jesus Christ. But make no mistake, my brothers; the adherents of a schismatic can never inherit the kingdom of God. Those who wander in outlandish by-ways of doctrine must forfeit all part in the Lord's Passion.

4. Make certain, therefore, that you all observe one common Eucharist;[1] for there is but one Body of our Lord Jesus Christ, and but one cup of union with His Blood, and one single altar of sacrifice – even as also there is but one bishop, with his clergy and my own fellow-servitors the deacons. This will ensure that all your doings are in full accord with the will of God.

5. My love for you, brothers, is overflowing, and I am only too happy to provide for your security like this – though it is not really I myself, but Jesus Christ. It is for His sake that I am in chains; though this privilege only increases my fears, since I am still so far from perfection. Nevertheless, your prayers will set the seal on my progress to God, and help me to the inheritance which a merciful Providence has promised for me. I am clinging for refuge to the Gospel message as though to the incarnate Christ, and to the Apostles [2] as the collective ministry of the Church. Not, indeed, that the Prophets do not have a place in our hearts as well, since they too proclaimed the Gospel in their preaching, and set their hopes on Him. They waited in expectation of Him, and through their faith in Him they have obtained salvation within the unity of Jesus Christ. Such holy men merit our love and admiration; Jesus Christ has borne His own testimony to them, and they are included as participants in the universal Gospel hope.

6. All the same, if anyone should make use of them to propound Judaism to you, do not listen to him. Better hear talk of

Christianity from a man who is circumcised than of Judaism from one who is not – though in my judgement both of them alike, if they fail to preach Jesus Christ, are no more than tombstones and graves of the dead, which limit their inscriptions to the names of mere mortal men. Shun such knavish wiles and snares of the prince of this world, or else his arts will wear you down and weaken your love. Rather, come all of you to your meetings like one man, without a thought of disunity in your hearts.

I am thankful to say that, where you are concerned, my conscience is clear. Nobody can be bold enough to claim that I have ever been oppressive to a single one of you in any matter, great or small. I can only pray that none of those I spoke to may ever find the words I said rising up in evidence against him.[3]

7. It is true that some people did once take it into their heads to impose upon me,[4] in my unspiritual capacity. My spiritual self, however, no man can impose upon; for that comes from God, and its origin and its destination[5] are alike known to it, and it can bring hidden things to light. Thus, at the time I was with you,[6] I cried out, speaking with a loud voice – the very voice of God – 'Be loyal to your bishop and clergy and deacons'. Some who were there suspected me of saying this because I already knew of certain dissensions among you; but He whose prisoner I am will bear me witness that no such information had ever reached me from human lips. No; that was the preaching of the Spirit itself, telling you never to act in independence of the bishop, to keep your bodies as a temple of God, to cherish unity and shun divisions, and to be imitators of Jesus Christ as He was of His Father.

8. As for me, I did my part as one dedicated to the cause of unity; for where disunion and bad blood exist, God can never be dwelling. That is why the Lord offers forgiveness to all who repent, if their repentance brings them back into unity with God and with the bishop's council of clergy. I have the fullest confidence in the grace of Jesus Christ, that He will cast loose every chain that binds you; and I appeal to you not to let your actions

be prompted by any party spirit, but rather by the teaching of Christ.

Certain people declared in my hearing, 'Unless I can find a thing in our ancient records, I refuse to believe it in the Gospel'; and when I assured them that it is indeed in the ancient scriptures, they retorted, 'That has got to be proved'. But for my part, my records are Jesus Christ; for me, the sacrosanct records are His cross and death and resurrection, and the faith that comes through Him. And it is by these, and by the help of your prayers, that I am hoping to be justified.

9. The priests of old, I admit, were estimable men; but our own High Priest is greater, for He has been entrusted with the Holy of Holies,[7] and to Him alone are the secret things of God committed. He is the doorway to the Father, and it is by Him that Abraham and Isaac and Jacob and the prophets go in, no less than the Apostles and the whole Church; for all these have their part in God's unity. Nevertheless, the Gospel has a distinction all its own, in the advent of our Saviour Jesus Christ, and His Passion and Resurrection. We are fond of the prophets, and they did indeed point forward to Him in their preaching; yet it is the Gospel that sets the coping-stone on man's immortality. It is in all these different elements together that goodness resides, if you have a loving faith.

10. News has come to me that, in response to your prayers and your loving sympathy in Christ Jesus, peace now reigns in the church at Antioch in Syria. It would therefore be very fitting for you, as a church of God, to appoint one of your deacons to go there as God's ambassador, and when they are all assembled together to offer them your felicitations and give glory to the Name. The man whom you think suitable for such a mission will have the blessing of Jesus Christ, and at the same time it will also redound to your own glory. Granted that you have the goodwill, this is not too much for you to do for the Name of God — as their own near-by churches, who have sent their bishops, have already done, besides the others who sent clergy and deacons.

11. Philo,[8] the deacon from Cilicia who has been so well

spoken of, is at present giving me his help in preaching God's word. So too is Rheus Agathopous, one of the elect, who has followed after me from Syria, and abjured this earthly life. Both of them testify to the welcome they had from you, and I add my own gratitude to God for you. May you yourselves have no less a welcome from the Lord. As for certain persons who behaved uncivilly to them, may they be redeemed by the grace of Jesus Christ.

The brethren here at Troas send you their love and greetings. That is where I am writing this; and it will come to you by the hand of Burrhus,[9] whom the Ephesians and Smyrnaeans sent to bear me company, as a mark of honour. They themselves will be honoured by Jesus Christ, on whom they hope in body, soul and spirit, with faith and love and singleness of mind.

> Farewell to you in Jesus
> Christ, the Hope of us all.

NOTES

1. It was the custom of the sectaries to hold separate eucharistic services of their own.

2. Commentators differ about the interpretation of this word, as coupled here with the 'Gospel'. Some think it means what we call the 'Epistles' of the New Testament (so Ussher, Pearson, and Westcott). Zahn and others, on the other hand, believe that Ignatius has already included in his mind the (written) Gospels and Epistles under the single term 'the Gospel', and is now speaking of the Apostles as the personal expounders of them. Lightfoot however, argues that 'the Gospel' here does not mean a written document at all, but simply the evangelic message, and that 'the Apostles', taken in conjunction with the mention of 'the Prophets' in the next sentence, signifies the scriptures of the New and Old Testaments respectively.

3. Some of his utterances had apparently been maliciously represented as an attempt to stifle the free expression of opinion. His meaning here seems to be that they might be remembered against his detractors at the Judgement.

4. Evidently he had been the victim of some deception in his every-

day affairs. In the province of the spirit, however, he insists that deception is impossible.

5. Its origin and its destination. Clearly a recollection of *John* iii, 8: *thou canst not tell whence it cometh, and whither it goeth* (though the particular relevance here is not easy to see). This is one of several indications that the Fourth Gospel was known to Ignatius.

6. This shows that Ignatius and his party, after leaving Laodicea, instead of continuing westward along the main highway to Ephesus, must have branched off by the more northerly road which led them by way of Philadelphia and Sardis to Smyrna. (See the map on page 62.)

7. Entrance to the Holy of Holies was the prerogative of the Jewish High Priest alone. *The secret things of God* is an allusion to the sacred treasures (the ark of the covenant, the tables of the Law, the pot of manna, and Aaron's rod), to which only the priests had access.

8. He and Rheus Agathopous had caught up with Ignatius at Troas, after following him from Antioch; most probably with the news of the restoration of peace there. On their way through they had received hospitality at Philadelphia (and also at Smyrna; *Smyrnaeans* 10); though it appears that the heretics there had shown them some incivility.

9. See note 2 on *Ephesians* 2.

*

THE EPISTLE TO THE
SMYRNAEANS

*

This letter, like that to the Philadelphians, was written from Troas, and contains grateful allusions to the welcome given to Ignatius during his recent sojourn in Smyrna. Its chief concern, however, is to combat the perils of Docetism, which he had observed to be rife in the city. There is also a strong condemnation of the separatism which is bred by such heresies, and a more vigorous insistence than usual upon the duty of maintaining unity.

From IGNATIUS,
whose other name is Theophorus,

> To the church of God the Father and our
> beloved Jesus Christ at SMYRNA, *in Asia,*
> *mercifully endowed with all the gifts of the*
> *Spirit, filled with faith and love, lacking no*
> *spiritual grace, and a most reverend bearer of*
> *heavenly treasures.*[1]

All happiness to you, in purity of
spirit and in the word of God.

1. Glory be to Jesus Christ, the Divine One who has gifted you
with such wisdom. I have seen how immovably settled in faith
you are; nailed body and soul, as it were, to the cross of the
Lord Jesus Christ, and rooted and grounded in love by His
blood. You hold the firmest convictions about our Lord; believing Him to be truly of David's line in His manhood, yet Son of
God by the Divine will and power; truly born of a Virgin; baptized by John for His fulfilling of all righteousness; and in the
days of Pontius Pilate and Herod the Tetrarch truly pierced by
nails in His human flesh (a Fruit imparting life to us[2] from
His most blessed Passion), so that by His resurrection He might
set up a beacon[3] for all time to call together His saints and believers, whether Jews or Gentiles, in the one body of His
Church.

2. All this He submitted to for our sakes, that salvation might
be ours. And suffer He did, verily and indeed; just as He did
verily and indeed raise Himself again. His Passion was no unreal illusion, as some sceptics aver who are all unreality themselves. The fate of those wretches will match their belief, for one
day they will similarly become phantoms without substance
themselves.

3. For my own part, I know and believe that He was in
actual human flesh, even after His resurrection. When He appeared to Peter and his companions, He said to them, 'Take
hold of me; touch me, and see that I am no bodiless phantom'.
And they touched Him then and there, and believed, for they

had had contact with the flesh-and-blood reality of Him. That was how they came by their contempt for death, and proved themselves superior to it. Moreover, He ate and drank with them after He was risen, like any natural man, though even then He and the Father were spiritually one.

4. I caution you in this way, dear friends, though I am well aware that your conviction is as firm as my own; but I would fain protect you in advance against certain beasts of prey in human form. If you can, you should avoid all contact with these persons, much less give them any sort of acceptance. Confine yourselves simply to saying a prayer for them, in the hope that they may come to a better frame of mind (no easy thing to bring about, but Jesus Christ our true Life has the power to do it). After all, if everything our Lord did was only illusion, then these chains of mine must be illusory too! Also, to what end have I given myself up to perish by fire or sword or savage beasts? [4] Simply because when I am close to the sword I am close to God, and when I am surrounded by the lions I am surrounded by God. But it is only in the name of Jesus Christ, and for the sake of sharing His sufferings, that I could face all this; for He, the perfect Man, gives me strength to do so.

5. Yet there are some who in their blindness still reject Him — or rather are rejected by Him, since in fact what they are contending for is not so much the truth about Him as their own final extinction.[5] They refuse to be persuaded by the prophets, or the Law of Moses, or even in our own times by the Gospel — still less by the personal sufferings of so many of our own people, since they apply the same sort of argument to ourselves.[6] So what is the point of my standing well in the opinion of a man who blasphemes my Lord by denying that He ever bore a real human body? In saying that, he denies everything else about Him; and the body he himself is bearing must be nothing but a corpse.[7] My pen declines to write the names of these infidels, and I would even wish to have them erased from my memory altogether until such time as they come to a better mind about the Passion which effects our resurrection from the dead.

6. For let nobody be under any delusion; there is judgement in store even for the hosts of heaven, the very angels in glory, the visible and invisible powers themselves, if they have no faith in the blood of Christ. Let him who can, absorb this truth. High position is no excuse for pride; it is faith and love that are everything, and these must come before all else. But look at the men who have those perverted notions about the grace of Jesus Christ which has come down to us, and see how contrary to the mind of God they are. They have no care for love, no thought for the widow and orphan, none at all for the afflicted, the captive, the hungry or the thirsty.

7. They even absent themselves from the Eucharist and the public prayers, because they will not admit that the Eucharist is the self-same body of our Saviour Jesus Christ which suffered for our sins, and which the Father in His goodness afterwards raised up again. Consequently, since they reject God's good gifts, they are doomed in their disputatiousness. They would have done better to learn charity, if they were ever to know any resurrection. For us, the only proper course is to have no dealings whatever with men of that kind, and to avoid all mention of them either publicly or in private; reserving our attention for the prophets instead, and particularly for the Gospel, in which the Passion and the crowning glory of the Resurrection are unfolded before us.

8. Abjure all factions,[8] for they are the beginning of evils. Follow your bishop, every one of you, as obediently as Jesus Christ followed the Father. Obey your clergy too, as you would the Apostles; give your deacons the same reverence that you would to a command from God. Make sure that no step affecting the church is ever taken by anyone without the bishop's sanction. The sole Eucharist you should consider valid is one that is celebrated by the bishop himself, or by some person authorized by him. Where the bishop is to be seen, there let all his people be; just as wherever Jesus Christ is present, we have the world-wide Church. Nor is it permissible to conduct baptisms or love-feasts without the bishop. On the other hand, whatever does have his sanction can be sure of God's approval

too. This is the way to make certain of the soundness and validity of anything you do.

9. From now onwards the sensible thing would be to get back to our right minds while there is still time to repent and turn to God. You have only to acknowledge God and the bishop, and all is well; for a man who honours his bishop is himself honoured by God, but to go behind the bishop's back is to be a servant of the devil.

So then, may grace overflow in all your actions, as you rightly deserve. You have given me much comfort in every way, and may Jesus Christ do as much for you. Absent or present, I have had your love; and may God reward you for it. Do but endure all things for His sake, and you will attain to Him in the end.

10. The welcome you gave to Philo and Rheus Agathopous[9] as ministers of God (who have followed me here in His cause) was a credit to you. They give thanks to the Lord on your account, for all your goodness to them; and be sure you will lose nothing by it. My life is a humble offering for you; and so are these chains of mine, for which you never showed the least contempt or shame. Neither will Jesus Christ in His perfect loyalty show Himself ashamed of you.

11. The prayers that sped out from you have alighted upon the church at Antioch[10] in Syria (where I have come from, to salute everyone in my lordly fetters. Not that I deserve my membership there, for I am the very last of them all; but it is a privilege which the Divine Will has accorded me. Myself, I had no part in it; it was all due to the grace of God – grace which I am now praying to be given in fullest measure, so that with the help of your prayers I can make my way to Him). Therefore, to set the seal of perfection on your work both here and hereafter, it would be most fitting and would do much honour to God if your church were to appoint someone to go as His ambassador to Syria with your felicitations on the restoration of peace, on the recovery of their proper numbers, and on their re-establishment as a corporate body again. For my thought is that it would be well worth your while to send a letter by one of your people, joining them in giving glory to God for

the tranquillity He has granted them, and for the fact that through your prayers they have come safely to harbour at last. Since you are spiritually quite mature, pray think maturely now; and if the will to do well is yours, God will be ready enough to supply the means.

12. The brethren here in Troas send you their loving greetings. This letter comes to you from there by the hand of Burrhus, whom you and brethren of Ephesus have jointly sent as a companion for me. He has been the greatest solace to me in every way; I wish that everyone else could be like him, for he is the perfect pattern of the sacred ministry, and the favour of God will surely reward him richly. My greetings to your sainted bishop, to the reverend clergy, to my fellow-servitors the deacons, and to each and every one of you all in the name of Jesus Christ, in His flesh and blood, in the Passion and Resurrection of His Body and His Spirit, in the Divine Unity, and in your own unity also. Grace, mercy, peace and patience be with you, now and always.

13. Greeting too, to the families of my brethren who have wives and children; and to those virgins whom you call widows.[11] Farewell to you, in the power of the Father. Philo, who is here with me, adds his own greetings. Salutations to Tavia and her family; I am praying for that faithful and loving steadfastness of hers, both in the worldly and in the spiritual life. Greetings to Alce,[12] who is specially dear to me, and to the incomparable Daphnus, and Eutecnus, and all the others.

Farewell to you, in the
Grace of God.

NOTES

1. For this metaphor see note on *Ephesians* 9. Here the treasures are the qualities of the Christian character.

2. The Tree of Calvary is likened by more than one of the early Fathers to the Tree of Life which was planted in Paradise.

3. An allusion to *Isaiah* xlix, 22.

4. Ignatius does not yet know how he is to meet his end, for any of these methods might be employed. Indeed, all three of them actually played a part in the execution of his brother-martyr Polycarp; he was first threatened with the lions, then burnt at the stake, and finally given the *coup de grâce* with a dagger.

5. Because the denial of Christ's immortality necessarily implies the denial of their own.

6. They claim that since the Passion itself is unreal, all suffering for Christ's sake must be vain and pointless.

7. Since he does not believe it can rise again after death.

8. As this sentence seems to belong more closely to what follows, I have copied the editors who place it here rather than at the end of the previous chapter.

9. See the note on *Philadelphians* 11.

10. This reference to the restored tranquillity of the Antiochene church – here gracefully attributed to the prayers of the Smyrnaeans – introduces the ensuing proposal for the dispatch of a congratulatory message.

11. Either unmarried women included in the widows' register for purposes of charity, or perhaps actual widows whom because of their purity and devotion Ignatius characterizes as virgins.

12. Alce is remembered in the same affectionate way in the letter to Polycarp. An Alce, who may well be the same person, is mentioned many years later in the *Martyrdom of Polycarp* as a relative of Herod, the Smyrnaean official responsible for the martyr's arrest.

THE EPISTLE TO
POLYCARP

Together with his general letter to the Christians at Smyrna, Ignatius sent this short personal one to their bishop Polycarp, for whom he had formed a warm affection during his visit to the city. (Polycarp's own subsequent letter to the Philippians shows, incidentally, that this affection was returned in full measure.) Ignatius was considerably the older of the two men, and accordingly the admonitions he gives to his young friend are frank and outspoken. In the later sections he turns to address the Smyrnaean congregation collectively, exhorting them to maintain vigour and unity in their spiritual warfare.

From IGNATIUS,
whose other name is Theophorus.

> *My most cordial greetings to* POLYCARP,
> *who is bishop over the Smyrnaean church – or*
> *rather, who has God the Father for bishop over*
> *him, together with the Lord Jesus Christ.*

1. Since I had been impressed by the godly qualities of your mind – anchored, as it seemed, to an unshakable rock – it gave me much pleasure to set eyes on your sainted countenance (may God give me joy of it). But let me charge you to press on even more strenuously in your course, in all the grace with which you are clothed, and to call all your people to salvation. You must do justice to your position, by showing the greatest diligence both in its temporal and spiritual duties. Give thought especially to unity, for there is nothing more important than this. Make yourself the support of all and sundry, as the Lord is to you, and continue to bear lovingly with them all, as you are doing at present. Spend your time in constant prayer, and beg for ever larger gifts of wisdom. Be watchful and unsleeping in spirit. Address yourself to people personally, as is the way of God Himself, and carry the infirmities of them all on your own shoulders, as a good champion of Christ ought to do. The heavier the labour, the richer the reward.

2. There is no credit in spending all your affection on the cream of your pupils. Try rather to bring the more troublesome ones to order, by using gentleness. Nobody can heal every wound with the same unguent; where there are acute spasms of pain, we have to apply soothing poultices. So in all circumstances be *wise as the serpent*, though always *harmless as the dove*. The very reason you are given a body as well as a soul is to help you to gain the favour of this outward and visible world; though at the same time you must also pray for insight into the invisible world as well, so that you may come short of nothing and the whole treasury of the Spirit may be yours. Critical times like these need you, as the barque needs a helms-

127

man * or the storm-tossed mariner a haven, if men are ever to find their way to God. So be strict with yourself, like a good athlete of God. The prize, as well you know, is immortality and eternal life. I am offering myself, and these chains you cherished so affectionately, as a humble sacrifice on your behalf.

3. You must not let yourself be upset by those who put forward their perverse teachings so plausibly. Stand your ground with firmness, like an anvil under the hammer. The mark of a true champion is to stand up to punishment and still come off victorious. It is our duty, particularly when it is in God's cause, to accept trials of all kinds, if we ourselves are to be accepted by Him. So redouble your efforts, and watch out for every opportunity; but also keep your eyes on Him who has no need of opportunities, being outside all time.

> Whom no senses can reveal
> Was for us made manifest;
> Who no ache or pain can feel
> Was for us by pain opprest;
> Willing all thing to endure,
> Our salvation to procure.[1]

4. Take care that widows are not neglected; next to the Lord, be yourself their guardian. See that nothing is ever done without consulting you, and do nothing yourself without consulting God – as I am sure you never do. Take a firm stand. Hold services more frequently, and hunt up everyone by name. You must not be overbearing in your manner to slaves, whether men or women; but on the other hand, never let them get above themselves. It should be their aim to be better slaves, for the glory of God; so that they may earn a richer freedom at His hands. And they are not to set their hearts on gaining their liberty at the church's expense,[2] for then they only become slaves to their own longings.

5. Be wary of the devices of sinful men;[3] go further, and preach publicly against them. Tell my sisters to love the Lord,

* Adopting Lightfoot's conjectural emendation, to make the best sense of a dubious text.

and to content themselves physically and spiritually with their own husbands. Similarly, charge my brothers in the name of Jesus Christ to love their wives as the Lord loves the Church. If somebody is capable of passing all his days in chastity, in honour of the Lord's body, let him do so without any boasting; for if he boasts of it, he is lost, and if the news gets beyond the bishop's ears it is all over with his chastity. When men and women marry, it is desirable to have the bishop's consent to their union, so that the wedding may be a tribute to the Lord and not to their own carnal desire. The honour of God should be the aim in everything.

6. Pay careful regard to your bishop,[4] if you wish God to pay regard to you. My heart warms to men who are obedient to their bishop and clergy and deacons, and I pray for a place in heaven at their side. For everyone must work together in unison at this training of ours; comrades in its wrestling and racing, comrades in its aches and pains, comrades in its resting and in its rising, like God's good stewards and coadjutors and assistants. Make every effort to satisfy the Commander under whom you serve, and from whom you will draw your pay; and be sure that no deserter is found in your ranks. For a shield take your baptism, for a helmet your faith, for a spear your love, and for body-armour your patient endurance; and lay up a store of good works as a soldier deposits his savings,[5] so that one day you may draw the credits that will be due to you. And be patient and gentle with one another, as God is with you. Now and always, may you be a joy to me.

7. The news that thanks to your prayers things have quietened down in the church at Syrian Antioch has eased my mind greatly. It is a God-sent relief from all my anxieties – so long as my sufferings give me a passport to God in the end, and through your intercessions I can be found a true disciple.

And now, most blessed Polycarp, it would be eminently fitting if you were to summon the reverend members of your council and choose some generally approved person, known for his enterprise, who could be appointed as a courier for God. Commission this man to glorify God and add lustre to your own unwearied affection by making the journey to Syria.[6] A Christian, after all, is not his own master; he puts his time at God's disposal. This is one of God's good works; and it will be one of your own too, when completed – for I have every confidence in His grace and in your readiness for a meritorious action in His cause. I need waste no more words on this suggestion, for I know how fervently sincere you are.

8. As I have to leave Troas by sea for Neapolis at any moment (so the Divine will has ordered it), it is impossible for me to write to all the churches myself; so will you, as one who possesses the mind of God, write ahead to the churches along the route [7] and ask them to follow the same procedure? Those who are able can send emissaries of their own, and the others could forward their letters by your messengers; and thus the action will confer lasting honour on all of you. You are the fitting person for this task.

My good wishes to you all; and also to the Procurator's [8] lady, with her whole household, and her children's too. Remember me to my dear Attalus. Give my salutations to the fortunate man chosen for the Syrian journey; the grace of God will go with him all the time – and with Polycarp as well, for having sent him.

Farewell always in our God Jesus Christ. Rest in Him, in the unity and under the oversight of God. Remember me to Alce,[9] that very dear person.

Farewell in the Lord.

NOTES

1. Whom no senses can reveal ... etc. See note on *Ephesians* 7.

2. According to the *Apostolic Constitutions* one of the purposes for which church funds might be used was to purchase the emancipation of Christian slaves.

3. Apparently here, as certainly in *Philadelphians* 2, a reference to the teachers of heresy.

4. At this point the personal letter to Polycarp changes abruptly

into a public exhortation to the whole Smyrnaean community. The sudden alteration is curious. May it perhaps have something to do with the haste and confusion in which all these epistles were composed?

5. Donatives, prize money, and other items over and above a soldier's regular pay were deposited in his name in the regimental savings bank, and handed to him at the conclusion of his service.

6. For the purpose of expressing the Smyrnaean church's joy at the restoration of tranquillity in Antioch, news of which had just been brought to Ignatius by the messengers Philo and Agathopous. In the accompanying letter to the Smyrnaean congregation he repeats this request, which he also makes in his letter to the Philadelphians. (In the earlier four letters written at Smyrna, before the news had reached him, he had only asked that prayers should be offered for his afflicted Antiochenes.)

7. The churches on the messenger's route from Smyrna to Antioch, such as Colossae, the Pisidian Antioch, Iconium, and others. In imagination Ignatius is viewing the road to the East through the eyes of the letter-carrier himself.

8. In the Greek, *Epitropus*. As this is a very rare proper name, it seems more likely to be used here (as it is in certain inscriptions which have been found at Smyrna) as the title of an official.

9. See the note on *Smyrnaeans* 13.

*

THE EPISTLE OF POLYCARP
TO THE
PHILIPPIANS

*

Polycarp of Smyrna

Side by side with Ignatius of Antioch in the sub-apostolic firmament, there shines his twin star Polycarp of Smyrna. Thanks to his pupil Irenaeus, we know slightly more of Polycarp than we do of Ignatius, but only enough to give us a tantalizing glimpse or two of his long pilgrimage from boyhood to old age. There is an account of his life, full of miracles and legends, which is attributed to the fourth-century writer Pionius; but however edifying it may be to the pious, it is of little or no historical worth. If we accept the view – which we shall discuss in a moment – that his martyrdom took place in A.D. 155, it will follow that he was born in 69 or 70, since at his death he speaks of himself as 'having served Christ for eighty-six years'. No doubt those words might possibly have been a reference to his conversion rather than his birth, but as this would increase his age to an altogether unlikely extent, the simpler interpretation is the more natural. If we understand them so, they also of course carry the implication that he was born of Christian parents. Irenaeus tells us that the youthful Polycarp had been 'instructed by Apostles, and had had familiar intercourse with many who had seen Christ'.* His long life thus makes him an invaluable link joining the teachers and theologians of the late second century to the doctrines and traditions of the earliest founders of the Church.

So far as is known, Polycarp was a native of the Roman proconsular province of Asia,† and lived all his life there. During his youth this province had become the heart of the Christian world, for before the fall of Jerusalem in A.D. 70 numbers of Church leaders and their followers had left the Holy Land and come to settle in the cities of Asia. In particular, the last surviving Apostle, St John, had made his home in Ephesus, and his name and influence had become a magnet for

* *Haer*. iii, 3, 4.
† This consisted of the districts of Mysia, Lydia, Caria and Phrygia.

all that was most vital in Christendom. The young Polycarp himself was one of his disciples, and in later life was fond of recalling his precious memories of the saint. According to Tertullian,* it was from St John that he received his appointment to the bishopric of Smyrna, but there is no other evidence of the truth of this. More probably it was the Smyrnaean bishop Bucolus who chose him as his successor.

Smyrna, the only one of the great coastal cities of Asia Minor which has survived to this day, is of immense antiquity. Its records run back in an unbroken line to the dawn of history, and it claims to have been the birthplace of Homer. Under the Romans, by whom it was specially favoured on account of its assistance to them in the Mithridatic wars, it was among the busiest and most prosperous trading centres of the Empire. Precisely when the first Christian church was planted there is uncertain; but some fifteen years before Polycarp's birth St Paul had stayed for three years in Ephesus, and we are told that during that period 'all those who dwelt in Asia heard the word of God'.† Presumably therefore it was at that time that the church in Smyrna had been established. But there can have been little ease for its pastors either then or afterwards. The religious world of that era was the scene of tumultuous struggles between conflicting creeds and cults. Paganism, encouraged by imperial authority, was experiencing a vigorous and militant revival. As Renan has observed, 'we are too forgetful that the second century saw a veritable pagan propaganda parallel to that of Christianity'. New temples, priesthoods, rites and festivals were springing up; astrology, sorcery, dreams and omens revived and flourished; and in all this Smyrna took a prominent part. It was also the chief Asian centre of the State-cult; Rome, the Senate, the emperor all figured as deities on its coins and inscriptions. Mithraism too, and a swarm of exotic religions from Syria and Egypt made their home in the city. Furthermore, in addition to the hostility of paganism, the Christian flock was also plagued from its earliest days by the bitter malevolence of the strong Jewish colony. In the Book of Revela-

* *Praescript.* 32.   † *Acts* xix, 10.

tion the struggling church of Smyrna is addressed with the words
*I know thy tribulations and thy poverty (but thou art rich), and
the blasphemy of them which say they are Jews, and are not, but
are a synagogue of Satan.** Many years after those words had
been written, the same persistent Jewish fanaticism was busy
piling faggots together for the martyrdom of Polycarp.

Added to these two sources of trouble was a third. For not
only was the church beset from without, by paganism on the
one hand and Jewry on the other; it was harassed from within
by schisms and dissensions. The various heresies which afterwards swelled to such many-headed proportions were beginning
to emerge from the cradle, and teachers were appearing everywhere with new and perverse doctrines. All these contributed
their share to the difficulties of Polycarp's episcopate.

Though he held the see of Smyrna for nearly half a century,
we know virtually nothing of his career in office. One small
incident is related in a letter of Irenaeus which Eusebius
quotes.† Not many months before his death Polycarp paid a
visit to Rome, and was amicably received there by the bishop
Anicetus. Among other matters which the two prelates dis-
cussed was the difference between their respective times of keeping Easter. Neither succeeded in changing the other's views, but
they parted on the friendliest terms, and the kindly Anicetus
allowed his visitor to preside at a celebration of the Eucharist.
This is the last glimpse we have of Polycarp's ministry; for soon
after his return to Smyrna a new persecution broke out, and
there were clamours for his arrest. He withdrew reluctantly to
a house in the country, which seems to have been his own
property, but he was traced and followed. Under torture one
of his servants betrayed his whereabouts. He offered no resistance to his captors, and was seized and taken back to the city.
A festival was in progress at Smyrna at the time, with public
games in the circus; and the aged bishop, together with eleven
other Christian victims, was condemned to die in the arena.
There he met his fate with calm dignity and unflinching courage, rejecting all attempts to persuade him to recant. The

* *Revelation* ii, 8.   † *H.E.* v, 24 (Penguin edition p. 233).

137

description of his martyrdom which was afterwards circulated by the Smyrnaean church is one of the treasures of early Christian literature.

Polycarp's name, which might be translated 'Mr Much-Fruit', aptly pictures his character for us: the type of humble, pious pastor whom John Bunyan would have delighted to draw. He had not, perhaps, much book-learning; he admits with humility that his knowledge of the Scriptures is not up to that of the Philippians. His writing is simple and direct, with no pretensions to literary style and none of the imagery and impetuosity of Ignatius. Unlike Ignatius again, he had a mind that was essentially uncreative; he could not originate, he could only transmit. But at least he could transmit faithfully, and it is this that explains the peculiar value of his witness. In an age when men were 'tossed to and fro and carried about with every wind of doctrine', Polycarp's steadfast reiteration of the truths he had learnt in youth were the greatest service he could have rendered to the Church. His beliefs were 'anchored to an unshakable rock', as Ignatius told him, and this single-minded fidelity ensured the continuity of the Apostolic faith as nothing else could have done. His simple piety caused him to react instinctively, by a sort of reflex action of the mind, to any form of heresy. When the notorious heretic Marcion accosted him on one occasion with the challenge, 'Recognize us', Polycarp's immediate rejoinder was, 'I recognize you as the first-born of Satan'; and in his later years the growth of false teaching so pained him that he is represented by Irenaeus as exclaiming, 'O good God, what sort of era hast thou preserved me for, that I have to suffer things like this!' *

In what year, and on what day, did his execution take place? A lot of interesting detective work has gone into the search for an answer to this question. Lightfoot, for example, devotes seventy-three pages to the problem. Until modern times nearly every writer was at least agreed on the year, which was assumed to be A.D. 167. This was on the supposed authority of Eusebius,

* Irenaeus (*Letter to Florinus*), quoted by Eusebius, *H.E.* v, 20 (Penguin edition, p. 228).

in whose *Chronological Tables* a note appended to the records of the emperor Marcus Aurelius's seventh year says, 'Persecution overtook the Church; Polycarp was martyred, and also in Gaul many suffered martyrdom bravely.' This is undoubtedly a reference to the notorious persecutions in Vienne and Lyons. But they took place, as we know, in 177; and the obvious inference is that Eusebius has simply happened to insert a general mention here of the various persecutions suffered by the Church while Aurelius was on the throne, and that he believed Polycarp's death to be one of the many that occurred during this reign. Unfortunately for his belief, the text of the *Martyrdom of Polycarp* states distinctly that the provincial governor at the time was a certain Statius Quadratus, and in the time of Aurelius there was no proconsul of that name in Asia. The question then turns on discovering the actual year in which Quadratus did hold office. No official record of this survives; but a possible clue has been unearthed among the writings of an obscure rhetorician called Aristides, who was a younger contemporary of Polycarp. In a panegyric on Aesculapius, the god of healing, this Aristides describes the progress of a long illness of his own, and in his narrative the name of Quadratus happens to be mentioned. In one place, after alluding to the proconsulship of one Severus (which we know to have been in 154), he speaks of 'the coming of Quadratus the rhetorician to govern Asia'; and a little later on we find him saying, 'Severus the governor of Asia held office, I think, the year before my colleague'. It is argued that this colleague must almost certainly have been his fellow-rhetorician Quadratus; and in that case the year of Quadratus' proconsulship – and with it Polycarp's martyrdom – becomes established as 155. Other years still continue to find their defenders, but on the whole this has now gained the widest acceptance. Complete certainty, for the present, must remain unobtainable.

The problem of determining the day itself is equally complex, and much critical ingenuity has been spent on finding a solution. The text of the *Martyrdom* says that Polycarp met his death 'on the second day of the first fortnight of Xanthicus, seven days before the kalends of March, two hours after midday on the Greater Sabbath'. Here the writer has taken pains to give us three distinct means of identifying the date, by references respectively to the Syrian, Roman, and Jewish systems of reckoning. To take the Syrian first, there exists in the Medicean Library an ancient manuscript setting out the comparison of various local calendars with the Roman; and one of these, the so-called 'Ephesian' calendar, shows the Syrian month Xanthicus as having two 'firsts', the 21st and 22nd of February.* In that case 'the second day of the first fortnight of Xanthicus' would be February 23rd; and this is also confirmed by the statement that in Roman reckoning it was 'seven days before the kalends of March'. So far, then, so good; but we are still left with the question of the Greater Sabbath. In the year 155 the 23rd of February did, in fact, fall on a Saturday, or sabbath (which is part of the case for favouring that year rather than 167), but why is it called a Greater Sabbath? That would presumably be a sabbath that happened to coincide with some high day or festival; and the most probable conjecture is that in this particular instance it may have been the great Hebrew feast of Purim. In Polycarp's time the Jewish calendar had not yet been officially stabilized, but varied from place to place; and though the assumption cannot be verified, there is nothing unreasonable in surmising that on the 23rd of February in 155 the Jewish community of Smyrna may have been keeping the feast of Purim.

But even so we are not out of the wood. For we have also to remember that when Polycarp was martyred in the arena, there was a heathen municipal festival in progress. What celebrations could have been taking place on February 23rd? Here again there is only conjecture to help us. Of three important Smyrnaean festivals that we know about, the likeliest seems to be that of the Asian Confederation, the body responsible for fostering and supervising the cult of emperor-worship throughout the province.† We happen to know, from an inscription found at Ephesus, that the eighth day before the kalends of

* The day is repeated because of a local superstition that the last day of every month must be the 'thirtieth'.
† See note 17 on *Martyrdom* 12.

March (that is, February 22nd) was called 'Caesar's Day', and this strongly suggests that it was a probable time for holding the Confederation games, which generally lasted for several days. An additional point is that the city of Smyrna was the chief provincial centre of the emperor-cult, and when it was the turn of the Confederation games to be celebrated there, they were on a more than usually elaborate scale. This would account for the joint presence in the theatre of both the Proconsul and the Asiarch, which we read of in the *Martyrdom*.

When all is said and done, however, we have only intelligent guesswork to guide us in all this. We must still wait for further evidence before the problems are satisfactorily solved. In the meantime it may be noted that the universal tradition of the Greek Orthodox Church commemorates Polycarp's decease on February 23rd. In the Church of Rome, on the other hand, it is observed on January 26th; but this is apparently due to confusing our Polycarp with a namesake of his from Nicaea, who also met a martyr's death.

THE EPISTLE OF POLYCARP

The Roman colony of Philippi was a flourishing and important city in southern Macedonia on the Via Egnatia, the Great East Road which led from Rome into Asia. As it was at no great distance from Neapolis, the port at which their ship had arrived from Troas, the guards of Ignatius had found it a natural and convenient place at which to break their long journey into Italy. During this short halt Ignatius had requested the local Christians (as he had also requested other communities along his route) to send a fraternal letter to his own church at Antioch in Syria, expressing their happiness that the troubles there had come to an end. It is possible that he may have named the bishop of Smyrna as one who had already agreed to do this; at all events, when the Philippians had written the desired letter they sent it to Polycarp at Smyrna, asking him as a favour to have it dispatched to Antioch along with his own. At the same time they begged to see the Smyrnaeans' own letter from Ignatius,

and also any other letters of his which Polycarp might possess.
The present epistle is Polycarp's reply. It is the only example
of his writings that has come down to us. The Philippians, it
seems, had intimated that they would welcome any spiritual
counsels or exhortations from him, and accordingly these occupy
the greater part of the letter. The most earnest of his warnings
are directed against the love of money, which had recently been
the downfall of one of their church officials, and against the
Docetist heretics who denied the reality of Christ's incarnation.
In addition, there are notes on the duties of presbyters and
deacons, and of Christian laymen and women. The letter ends
with his promise to forward their fraternal message to Antioch;
there is even a chance, he says, that he may be going there himself, and in that case he will deliver it personally. He also en-
closes a packet of the Ignatian letters they had asked for.

No citations from the Old Testament are made in the epistle.
There are quotations from, or apparent allusions to, *Matthew,
Acts, Romans I, Corinthians, Galatians, Ephesians, II Thessa-
lonians, I Timothy*, and *I Peter*, but nothing indicates that he
ascribed Scriptural authority to them. In striking contrast to the
Ignatian stress on episcopacy, Polycarp makes no mention at all
of the bishop. This may mean that there was no bishop at
Philippi at the time; or, as some think, it may be because bishops
had not yet everywhere come to be distinguished from presbyters. In support of the latter theory, the letter of Clement is
quoted as evidence for the identity of bishops and presbyters,
and it is also pointed out that the duties which Polycarp assigns
here to the presbyters are those which other writers elsewhere
attribute to bishops. Curiously, the duty of preaching is not included by Polycarp among these responsibilities.

We have no indication of the date of the epistle except what
can be inferred from its contents; and here we find ourselves in
a dilemma. On the one hand, the allusion in chapter 9 to Ignatius and his fellow-martyrs as having 'run their course' and being 'in their well-earned place at the Lord's side' implies that the
fact of their death was already known to Polycarp. Later on,
however, his request in chapter 13 for the latest news of them

suggests that they were still on their way from Philippi to Rome.* This apparent contradiction prompted P. N. Harrison in 1936 to put forward the attractive theory that our present text is in reality a combination of two quite different letters. In his assumption, chapter 13 is the earlier of these, being no more than a brief covering note to enclose the documents requested by the Philippians, and written before Ignatius and his party had had time to reach Rome. The preceding twelve chapters would then represent a very much later letter, written some twenty-five years afterwards on the occasion of a crisis in the Philippian church.

The Greek text of the epistle is incomplete, breaking off at the end of the ninth chapter. For the remainder we have to rely on a subsequent Latin translation.

* Both these chapters are reproduced by Eusebius, *H.E.* iii, 36 (Penguin edition, p. 147).

All mercy and peace to you, from
God Almighty and Jesus Christ our
Saviour.

1. When you welcomed those copies of the True Love,[1] and took the opportunity of setting them forward on their road, it made me as happy in Jesus Christ as it did you. For those chains they were wearing were the badges of saints; the diadems of men truly chosen by God and our Lord. It does my heart good to see how the solid roots of your faith, which have had such a reputation ever since early times, are still flourishing and bearing fruit for Jesus Christ. In Him, endurance went so far as to face even death for our sins; but God overruled the pangs of the grave, and raised Him up to life again. Though you never saw Him for yourselves, yet you believe in Him in a glory of joy beyond all words (which not a few others would be glad to share), well knowing that it is by His grace you are saved, not of you own doing but by the will of God through Jesus Christ.

2. So gird up your loins now and serve God in fear and sincerity. No more of the vapid discourses and sophistries of the vulgar;[2] put your trust in Him who raised our Lord Jesus Christ from the dead, and gave Him glory and a seat at His own right hand. All things in heaven and earth have been made subject to Him; everything that breathes pays Him homage; He comes to judge the living and the dead, and God will require His blood at the hands of any who refuse Him allegiance. And He that raised Him from the dead will raise us also, if we do His will and live by His commandments, and cherish the things He cherished – if, that is to say, we keep ourselves from wrongdoing, overreaching,[3] penny-pinching, tale-telling, and prevaricating, and bear in mind the words of our Lord in His teaching, *Judge not, that you be not judged; forgive, and you will be forgiven; be merciful, that you may obtain mercy; for whatever you*

144

measure out to other people will be measured back again to yourselves.* And again, *Happy are the poor and they who are persecuted because they are righteous, for theirs is the kingdom of God.†*

3. Not that I should be taking on myself to write to you in this way about the life of holiness, my brothers, if you yourselves had not invited me to do so. For I am as far as anyone else of my sort from having the wisdom of our blessed and glorious Paul. During his residence with you he gave the men of those days clear and sound instruction in the word of truth, while he was there in person among them; and even after his departure he still sent letters which, if you study them attentively, will enable you to make progress in the faith which was delivered to you. Faith is the mother of us all; with Hope following in her train, and Love of God and Christ and neighbour leading the way. Let a man's mind be wholly bent on these, and he has fulfilled all the demands of holiness; for to possess Love is to be beyond the reach of sin.

4. But troubles of every kind stem from the love of money. Therefore, since we know that *we brought nothing into this world, and we can carry nothing out,‡* we must gird on the armour of integrity, and the first step must be to school our own selves into conformity with the Divine commandments. After that we can go on to instruct our womenfolk in the traditions of the faith, and in love and purity; teaching them to show fondness and fidelity to their husbands, and a chaste and impartial affection for everyone else, and to bring up their children in the fear of God. Widows are to observe discretion as they practise our Lord's faith; they should make constant intercessions for everyone, and be careful to avoid any tale-bearing, spiteful tittle-tattle, false allegations, over-eagerness for money, or misconduct of any description. They are to recognize that they are an altar of God,[4] who scrutinizes every offering laid on it, and from whom none of their thoughts or intentions – no single one of their heart's secrets – can be hidden.

* *Matthew* vii, l. † ibid. v, 3. ‡ *I Timothy* vi, 7.

5. We know that *God is not mocked,** and therefore we owe it to ourselves to behave in a manner worthy of His precepts and His glory. By the same token, our deacons must never be open to any reproach at the bar of His righteousness, remembering that they are ministers of God and not of men. There must be no traducing of others, no paltering with the truth, no itching palms; they must be men utterly self-disciplined, humane and hard working, who pass their lives in the true spirit of the Lord who came to be the servant of us all. To please Him in this present world is to earn the world to come, for we have His promise that He will raise us from the grave; and if we prove ourselves good citizens of His here, we shall reign with him hereafter, if we have faith.

Our younger men, like the deacons, must be unspotted in all respects, making purity their first care and keeping a strict curb on any tendencies to loose living. In this world it is a good thing to make a clean break with all our carnal desires; because *all the lusts of the flesh are up in arms against the Spirit,*† and because *no fornicator, pervert, or sodomite will inherit the kingdom of God*‡ – nor anyone else of dissolute habits. Our duty, therefore, is to give everything of this kind a very wide berth, and be as obedient to our clergy and deacons as we should be to God and Christ. The conduct of our young women, equally, must show the unblemished purity of their conscience.

6. As for the clergy, they should be men of generous sympathies, with a wide compassion for humanity. It is their business to reclaim the wanderers, keep an eye on all who are infirm, and never neglect the widow, the orphan, or the needy. Their care at all times should be for what is honourable in the sight of God and men. Any show of ill-temper, partiality, or prejudice is to be scrupulously avoided; and eagerness for money should be a thing utterly alien to them. They must not be over ready to believe ill of anyone, nor too hasty with their censure; being well aware that we all of us owe the debt of sin. If we pray to the Lord to forgive us, we ourselves must be forgiving; we are all under the eyes of our Lord and God, and every one of us must

* *Galatians* vi, 7.   † ibid. v, 17.   ‡ *I Corinthians* vi, 9.

stand before the judgement-seat of Christ, where each will have to give an account of himself. Therefore let our serving of Him be marked by that fear and reverence which He Himself, no less than the Apostles who brought us the Gospel, and the Prophets who foretold the Lord's coming, has enjoined upon us. Let us have a real ardour for goodness, taking every care to avoid giving offence, and refusing all association with false brethren and those hypocritical bearers of the Lord's name who only lead empty heads astray.

7. To deny that Jesus Christ has come in the flesh is to be Antichrist. To contradict the evidence of the Cross is to be of the devil. And to pervert the Lord's words to suit our own wishes, by asserting that there are no such things as resurrection or judgement, is to be a first-begotten son of Satan. So let us have no more of this nonsense from the gutter, and these lying doctrines, and turn back again to the Word originally delivered to us. Let us *be sober and watch unto prayer,* * earnestly adjuring the all-seeing God to *lead us not into temptation*† – since, as the Lord has told us, *though the spirit is willing, the flesh is weak*.‡

8. Let us never relax our grasp on the Hope and Pledge of our righteousness; I mean Jesus Christ, *who bore our sins in his own body on the tree*; who *did no sin, neither was guile found in his mouth*§ who steadfastly endured all things for our sakes, that we might have life in Him. Let us imitate that patient endurance of His; and if we do have to suffer for His Name's sake, why then, let us give glory to Him. For that is the example He set us in His own person, and in which we have learnt to put our faith.

9. I appeal now to every one of you to hear and obey the call of holiness, and to exercise the same perfect fortitude that you have seen with your own eyes in the blessed Ignatius, and Rufus, and Zosimus; and not in them alone, but in a number of your own townsmen as well – to say nothing of Paul himself and the other Apostles. Be very sure that the course of these men was not run in vain, but faithfully and honourably; and that

* *I Peter* iv, 7.   † *Matthew* vi, 13.   ‡ *Matthew* xxvi, 41.
§ *I Peter* ii, 22, 24.

they have now reached a well-earned place at the side of the Lord whose pains they shared. Their hearts were not set on this world of ours, but on Him who died for our sakes, and was raised up again for us by God.

10.[5] Stand firm, then, in these ways, taking the Lord for your example. Be fixed and unshaken in your faith; care for each other with a brother's love, and make common cause for the truth. Give way to one another in the Lord's own spirit of courtesy, treating no one as an inferior. When it is in your power to do a kindness, never put it off to another time, for *charity is death's reprieve.** Let everyone respect his neighbour's rights, so that the heathen may have no occasion to find fault with your way of life. By so doing you will not only earn approval for the good you do, but you will avoid bringing the Lord into any disrepute. Woe betide anyone who does bring the Lord into disrepute; so impress upon everybody that they are to be as sober and sensible as you are yourselves.

11. My heart is sore for Valens,[6] sometime one of your clergy, that he should have so little understanding of the office that was conferred on him. It moves me to warn you earnestly against any excessive fondness for money, and to insist upon your absolute probity and integrity. You must keep yourselves from the slightest taint of wrong. If a man has no control over himself in matters of this sort, how can he possibly preach it to anyone else? If he fails to rise above the love of money, he will find himself corrupted by the worship of his idol, and be classed with the heathen who know nothing of the Divine judgement. *Do we not know*, Paul teaches us, *that it is God's people who are to judge the world?†* (I am not saying that I have seen or heard of anything of the sort among yourselves – you with whom the blessed Paul laboured, and who were his *letters of commendation‡* in those early days, and of whom he made his boast in all those churches where alone God was then known, in the time before we ourselves had received the knowledge of Him.[7]) I feel the deepest sorrow for that man and his wife; may the Lord grant them real repentance. You too, for your part, must not be

* *Tobit* xii, 9.   † *I Cor.* vi, 2.   ‡ *II Cor.* iii, 2.

over severe with them, for people of that kind are not to be looked on as enemies; you have to restore them, like parts of your own person that are ailing and going wrong, so that the whole body can be maintained in health. Do this, and you will be promoting your own spiritual welfare at the same time.

12. I have no doubt you are well versed in Holy Scripture, and that it holds no secrets for you (which is more than has been granted to me). Only, it says there, *Do not be angry to the point of sin; do not let the sun go down on your indignation.** The happy man is he who keeps this in mind, and I am sure that is true of you. May the God and Father of our Lord Jesus Christ, and the eternal High Priest Jesus Christ Himself, the Son of God, help you to grow in faith and truth, in unfailing gentleness and the avoidance of all anger, in patience and forbearance, and in calmness and purity. To you, and to ourselves as well, and to all those under heaven who shall one day come to believe in our Lord Jesus Christ and in His Father who raised Him from the dead, may He grant part and portion among His saints.

Pray for all God's people. Pray too for our sovereign lords, and for all governors and rulers; for any who ill-use you or dislike you; and for the enemies of the Cross. Thus the fruits of your faith will be plain for all to see, and you will be perfected in Him.

13. You and Ignatius have both written to me to ask whether anyone who may be going to Syria could deliver a letter from you there along with ours. I will see that this is done; perhaps by myself personally if I can find a suitable opportunity, or else by someone whom I will send to act for both of us. I am sending you Ignatius's letters, as you requested; the ones he wrote to us, and some others that we had in our possession. They are enclosed herewith; you will be able to derive a great deal of benefit from them, for they tell you all about faith, and perseverance, and all the ways of self improvement that involve our Lord. And if you should have any certain news of Ignatius himself and his companions, pray let us know.

* *Ephesians* iv, 26.

149

14. This goes to you by the hand of Crescens; I commended him to you some time ago, and I repeat the commendation now. His conduct here among us has been above reproach, and I am confident you will find it the same. You shall have a commendation for his sister too, when she reaches you.

Farewell to you and all your people, in the Lord Jesus Christ in grace.

NOTES

1. Ignatius and his fellow-prisoners, who had passed through Philippi on their way to martyrdom at Rome.
2. The myths and the philosophical speculations of the pagans; the legends and fables of the Jews; the theosophy of the Gnostics.
3. Besides its primary meaning of covetousness, this Greek word is a common euphemism in Christian writings for adultery. In the context here, however, the simpler sense is probably preferable.
4. Widows lived on the offerings of the faithful.
5. From this section onwards the Latin version is our only authority.
6. A presbyter who appears to have been guilty of some piece of financial dishonesty, in which his wife was also involved.
7. The evangelization of Smyrna was later than that of Philippi and other regions.

*

THE MARTYRDOM
OF
POLYCARP

*

The Martyrdom of Polycarp

Shortly after the death of Polycarp and his fellow martyrs, a request reached his bereaved congregation at Smyrna for a full account of the event. This came from members of the church at Philomelium, some two hundred miles away to the east in Phrygia; and there is an interesting conjecture that the apostate Quintus, whose defection is recorded in chapter four, himself came from that community. If so, their request may have been prompted by a desire to make some amends for the misconduct of their erring brother. However that may be, the Smyrnaeans agreed to do as they were asked; and accordingly a certain Marcion, who had been one of the eye-witnesses of the martyrdom, compiled for them this graphic description of the bishop's arrest and execution. They embodied it in the letter which they sent back to the Philomelians, with an intimation that it could also be circulated to other churches for their edification.

It is now generally acknowledged to be the earliest genuine record of the death of a Christian martyr that we possess. As such it has furnished a model for the innumerable pious martyrologies with which the Church's later literature abounds. The greater part of it was transcribed by Eusebius in his *History of the Church*,* though he omits one or two of the miraculous incidents.

Whoever Marcion was, he had the true story-teller's gift. From the opening account of Polycarp's fellow martyrs to the final collection of his calcined bones, the tale moves smoothly and swiftly without a wasted word. So vividly does he bring his scenes to life – the shrinking houseboy forced to guide the trackers to his master's hiding-place, the midnight arrest at the lonely country farm, the captured bishop serenely offering refreshments to his shamefaced captors – that we feel ourselves part of the drama. We flinch in sympathy when the old man barks his shins as he gets down from the police carriage, and

* *H.E.* iv, 15 (Penguin edition, pp. 168 ff).

admire his cheerful indifference to the hurt; and when prisoner and proconsul confront each other at last in the roaring circus, we share the pagan's bewilderment at the complete self-possession and calm rejoinders of the Christian. There is indeed something irresistibly attractive in the demeanour of this indomitable octogenarian – and the spell holds us, even to the final glimpse of the white-haired figure standing unscathed in the encircling flames 'like a loaf inside an oven'. The story has moved and thrilled readers in all ages; and we have the testimony of an eighteenth-century prelate that 'he knew not anything in all ecclesiastical antiquity that was more wont to affect his mind, and believed that no good Christian could be satisfied with reading it often enough'.

From the colony of God's Church[1]
at S M Y R N A,

> *To the colony of God's Church at* P H I L O-
> M E L I U M,[2] *and to all colonies of the Holy
> Catholic Church everywhere.*

*All mercy, peace, and love to you
from God the Father and our Lord
Jesus Christ.*

1. In this letter, brothers, we are sending you an account of the
martyrs, and in particular of the blessed Polycarp; whose witness
set the seal, so to speak, on the persecution and brought it to an
end. It was almost as though all the preceding events had been
leading up to another Divine manifestation of the Martyrdom
which we read of in the Gospel;[3] for Polycarp, just like the
Lord, had patiently awaited the hour of his betrayal – in token
that we too, taking our pattern from him, might think of others
before ourselves. This is surely the sign of a true and steadfast
love, when a man is not bent on saving himself alone, but his
brethren as well.

2. But indeed all the other martyrdoms that God willed to
take place (we must be careful to ascribe all things to His
governance) were blessed and noble. No one could fail to admire
their high-hearted endurance, and the love they showed for their
Master. Some of them were so cut to pieces by the scourges that
their very vitals were plainly exposed to view, down to the in-
most veins and arteries; and yet they still bore up, until even the
bystanders were moved to tears of pity for them. Others dis-
played such heroism that not a cry or a groan escaped from any
of them; which seemed a clear proof to us all that in that hour
of anguish those martyr-heroes of Christ were not present in the
body at all – or better still, that the Lord was standing at their
side and holding them in talk. So it was that, with all their
thoughts absorbed in the grace of Christ, they made light of the
cruelties of this world, and at the cost of a single hour purchased
for themselves life everlasting. For them, the fires of their bar-
barous tormentors had a grateful coolness, for they held ever

155

before their eyes their escape from the quenchless flames of eternity, and looking up they beheld with inward vision the good things in store for those who persevere. Things which *no eye has seen, no ear has heard, no mortal heart has dreamed of** were revealed by the Lord to those men – who by this time were men no longer, but already angels.

It was the same with those who were condemned to the wild beasts. The pains they endured were horrible, for they were forced to lie on beds of spikes and subjected to other varied forms of torture, in the hope that these lingering agonies would enable the Fiend to extort a recantation from them; in fact, there was no end to the devices the devil employed against them.

3. Thank God, however, all his efforts were unavailing. Germanicus, an example of true nobility, lent new strength to their failing spirits by his steadfast endurance. He confronted the savage beasts with the utmost gallantry, and when the Governor[4] attempted persuasion, urging him to have pity on his own youth, he even used force to drag the animal towards him, in his desire for a speedier release from that world of unjust and lawless men. It was then that the whole crowd, taken aback by the heroism which this brood of Christians, in their love and fear of God, were displaying, broke into yells of 'Down with the infidels![5] Go and find Polycarp!'

4. There was one man, however, Quintus by name, a Phrygian[6] recently arrived from Phrygia, whose courage failed him at the sight of the beasts. It was he who had compelled himself and some others to surrender themselves voluntarily; and after much persuasion he was induced by the Governor to take the oath and offer incense. (And that is the reason, brothers, why we do not approve of men offering themselves spontaneously. We are not taught anything of that kind in the Gospel.[7])

5. But the astonishing Polycarp, when he first heard the report, showed not the least sign of alarm, and was all for remaining in the city. However, the majority of us prevailed on him to leave, and so he made his way quietly to a small country property not far from the city. There he spent the time with

*I Cor. ii, 9 (Isaiah lxiv, 4).

a few friends, doing nothing else day and night but praying for us all, and for churches all over the world, as it was his usual habit to do. While he was thus at his prayers, three days before his arrest, he had a vision in which he saw flames reducing his pillow to ashes; whereupon he turned to his companions and said, 'I must be going to be burnt alive'.

6. As there was no sign of the search for him being abandoned, he then moved to another farm.[8] The searchers arrived hot on the heels of his departure, and when they failed to find him they arrested a couple of young houseboys, one of whom confessed under torture. (For after all, he could never have escaped detection. The circumstance that the traitors were men of his own household, and that the Police Commissioner[9] – to whom chance had even given the actual name of Herod – was resolved on bringing him into the arena, manifestly meant that he was to fulfil his destiny by sharing the experiences of Christ, and that his betrayers should likewise be doomed to the punishment of Judas.)

7. Tipstaffs and mounted policemen left at about supper-time on the Friday, taking the houseboy with them. The men had been issued with the regulation weapons, just as if it were a brigand they were tracking down.[10] They closed in on Polycarp late at night, and found him in bed in an attic. Even then he could have made his escape to another place, but he refused, saying, 'God's will be done'. As soon as he heard them arrive, he went down and chatted with them; and everyone there was struck by his age and his calmness, and surprised that the arrest of such an old man could be so urgent. In spite of the lateness of the hour he at once ordered them to be given all the food and drink they wanted; and then asked if he might be allowed an hour to pray undisturbed. When they consented, he got to his feet and prayed; so full of the grace of God, that two whole hours went by before he could bring himself to be silent again. All who heard him were struck with awe, and many of them began to regret this expedition against a man so old and saintly.

8. At length, when he had remembered everyone whom

chance had ever brought him into contact with – small and great, known and unknown – as well as the entire world-wide Catholic Church, he brought his prayer to an end. By then it was time to leave, so they mounted him on an ass [11] and took him to the city. That day was a Greater Sabbath;[12] and Herod, the Police Commissioner, accompanied by his father Nicetas, came out to meet him. They took him into their carriage, sat down beside him, and addressed him persuasively. 'Come now', they said, 'where is the harm in just saying "Caesar is Lord",[13] and offering the incense, and so forth, when it will save your life?' At first he made no reply, but when they kept on at him he said, 'No, I am not going to take your advice'. Then, after their efforts at persuasion had failed, they took to uttering threats; and they turned him out of the carriage so impatiently that he barked his shins as he was getting down. Without even turning his head, however, and as if nothing had happened, he stumped nimbly away at a brisk pace, as they led him towards the circus. Inside the circus itself there was now such an uproar going on that nobody could make himself heard.

9. As Polycarp stepped into the arena there came a voice from heaven, 'Be strong, Polycarp, and play the man'. No one caught sight of the speaker, but those of our friends who were there heard the voice. Finally he was brought forward for examination; and when the news spread round that it was Polycarp who had been captured, a deafening clamour broke out. He was brought before the Governor, who asked if this was the man; and when Polycarp admitted it, tried to persuade him to recant. 'Have some respect for your years', he said; adding the rest of the usual exhortations, 'Swear an oath "By the Luck of Caesar" [14] – Own yourself in the wrong, and say, "Down with the infidels!"' Polycarp's brow darkened as he threw a look round the turbulent crowd of heathens in the circus; and then, indicating them with a sweep of his hand, he said with a growl and a glance to heaven, 'Down with the infidels!'

The Governor, however, still went on pressing him. 'Take the oath, and I will let you go', he told him. 'Revile your Christ.' Polycarp's reply was, 'Eighty and six years have I served Him, and He has done me no wrong. How then can I blaspheme my King and my Saviour?'

10. Persisting in his attempts,[15] the Governor then said again, 'Swear by the Luck of Caesar.' He answered, 'If you still think I am going to swear by Caesar's Luck, and still pretend not to know what I am, let me tell you plainly now that I am a Christian; and if you want to know the meaning of Christianity, you have only to name a day and give me a hearing'. To this the Governor's reply was, 'Try your arguments on the crowd yonder'.[16] But Polycarp said, 'It is you whom I thought it might be worth discussing it with, because we have been taught to pay all proper respect to powers and authorities of God's appointment, so long as it does not compromise us. To defend myself to these people would only be a waste of time'.

11. The Governor then said, 'I have wild beasts here. Unless you change your mind, I shall have you thrown to them.' 'Why then, call them up', said Polycarp, 'for it is out of the question for us to exchange a good way of thinking for a bad one. It would be a very creditable thing, though, to change over from the wrong to the right'. The other said again, 'If you do not recant, I will have you burnt to death, since you think so lightly of wild beasts.' Polycarp rejoined, 'The fire you threaten me with cannot go on burning for very long; after a while it goes out. But what you are unaware of are the flames of future judgement and everlasting torment which are in store for the ungodly. Why do you go on wasting time? Bring out whatever you have a mind to.'

12. And all the time he was saying this and much else besides, he was overflowing with courage and joy, and his whole countenance was beaming with grace. It was not only that he himself was anything but prostrated with dismay at the threats which were uttered, it was the Governor who, on his part, found himself now completely at a loss. What he did next was to send his crier to give out three times, from the centre of the arena, 'Polycarp has admitted to being a Christian!' At the crier's words the whole audience, the heathens and the Jewish residents of Smyrna alike, broke into loud yells of ungovernable

fury: 'That teacher of Asia! That father-figure of the Christians! That destroyer of our gods, who is teaching whole multitudes to abstain from sacrificing to them or worshipping them!' Interspersed with shouts of this kind there were loud demands for the Asiarch [17] Philip to let loose a lion at Polycarp. However, he told them that the rules would not allow him to do this, since he had already declared the beast-fighting closed;[18] whereupon they decided to set up a unanimous outcry that he should have Polycarp burnt alive. (Thus was ensured the fulfilment of the vision he had had of his pillow, when he saw it catching fire during his prayers, and turned to his loyal friends with the prophetic words, 'I must be going to be burnt alive'.)

13. It was all done in less time than it takes to tell. In a moment the crowd had collected faggots and kindling from the workshops and baths; the Jews, as usual, being well to the fore with their help. When the pile was ready, he took off his outer garments, undid his girdle, and even tried to unfasten his shoes,[19] though he had never been accustomed to do this before, since the faithful used to vie with one another in their eagerness to touch his bare skin – such universal veneration had the saintliness of his life earned for him, even before his martyrdom. The irons with which the pyre was equipped were fastened round him; but when they proposed to nail him as well, he said, 'Let me be; He who gives me strength to endure the flames will give me strength not to flinch at the stake, without your making sure of it with nails'.

14. So they left out the nailing, and tied him instead. Bound like that, with his hands behind him, he was like a noble ram taken out of some great flock for sacrifice: a goodly burnt-offering all ready for God. Then he cast his eyes up to heaven and said:

'O Lord God Almighty, Father of thy blessed and beloved Son Jesus Christ, through whom we have been given knowledge of thyself; Thou art the God of angels and powers, of the whole creation, and of all the generations of the righteous who live in thy sight. I bless thee for granting me this day and hour, that I may be numbered amongst the martyrs, to share the cup of thine Anointed and to rise again unto life everlasting, both in body and soul, in the immortality of the Holy Spirit. May I be received among them this day in thy presence, a sacrifice rich and acceptable, even as thou didst appoint and foreshow, and dost now bring it to pass, for thou art the God of truth and in thee is no falsehood. For this, and for all else besides, I praise thee, I bless thee, I glorify thee; through our eternal High Priest in heaven, thy beloved Son Jesus Christ, by whom and with whom be glory to thee and the Holy Ghost, now and for all ages to come. Amen'.

15. As the amen soared up and the prayer ended, the men at the fire set their lights to it, and a great sheet of flame blazed out. And then we who were privileged to witness it saw a wondrous sight; and we have been spared to tell it to the rest of you. The fire took on the shape of a hollow chamber, like a ship's sail when the wind fills it, and formed a wall round about the martyr's figure; and there was he in the centre of it, not like a human being in flames but like a loaf baking in the oven, or like a gold or silver ingot being refined in the furnace. And we became aware of a delicious fragrance, like the odour of incense or other precious gums.

16. Finally, when they realized that his body could not be destroyed by fire, the ruffians ordered one of the dagger-men [20] to go up and stab him with his weapon. As he did so, there flew out a dove,[21] together with such a copious rush of blood that the flames were extinguished; and this filled all the spectators with awe, to see the greatness of the difference that separates unbelievers from the elect of God. Of these last, the wondrous martyr Polycarp was most surely one: bishop of the Catholic Church at Smyrna, and a teacher in our own day who combined both apostle and prophet in his own person. For indeed, every word that ever fell from his lips either has had, or will have, its fulfilment.

17. But the jealous and envious Evil One, who always opposes the family of the righteous, and had noticed the sublimity of his martyrdom and the unspotted record of his life since its earliest days, now saw him in the act of having a crown of

immortality set upon his head, and bearing off a prize which none could dispute. He therefore proceeded to do his best to arrange that at least we should not get possession of his mortal remains, although numbers of us were anxious to do this and to claim our share in the hallowed relics. Accordingly he put it into the head of Nicetas (the father of Herod, and brother of Alce) to make an application to the Governor not to release the body; 'in case', he said, 'they should forsake the Crucified and take to worshipping this fellow instead'. This was said under strong pressure from the Jews, who had been observing us as we were about to draw it out of the fire. Little do they know that it could never be possible for us to abandon the Christ who died for the salvation of every soul that is to be saved in all the world – the Sinless One dying for sinners – or to worship any other. It is to Him, as the Son of God, that we give our adoration; while to the martyrs, as disciples and imitators of the Lord, we give the love they have earned by their matchless devotion to their King and Teacher. Pray God we too may come to share their company and their discipleship.

18. However, when the centurion saw that the Jews were spoiling for a quarrel, he had the body fetched out publicly,[22] as is their usage, and burnt. So, after all, we did gather up his bones – more precious to us than jewels, and finer than pure gold – and we laid them to rest in a spot suitable for the purpose.[23] There we shall assemble, as occasion allows, with glad rejoicings; and with the Lord's permission we shall celebrate the birthday of his martyrdom.[24] It will serve both as a commemoration of all who have triumphed before, and as a training and a preparation for any whose crown may be still to come.

19. Such then is the record of Polycarp the Blessed. Including those from Philadelphia, he was the twelfth to meet a martyr's death in Smyrna; though he is the only one to be singled out for universal remembrance and to be talked of everywhere, even in heathen circles. Not only was he a famous Doctor, he was a martyr without a peer; and one whose martyrdom all aspire to imitate, so fully does it accord with the Gospel of Christ. His

steadfastness proved more than a match for the Governor's injustice, and won him his immortal crown. Now, in the fullness of joy among the Apostles and all the hosts of heaven, he gives glory to the Almighty God and Father, and utters the praises of our Lord Jesus Christ – who is the Saviour of our souls, the Master of our bodies, and the Shepherd of the Catholic Church the wide world over.

20. We know that you asked us for a more exhaustive account of the events than this; but we have had this brief summary made by our brother Marcion [25] for you to be going on with. When you have finished reading it, send the letter on to your brethren further away, for them too to glorify the Lord who singles out His chosen saints from among the number of His bondsmen.

And now to Him whose plenteous grace is able to bring us all into His heavenly kingdom, through His only-begotten Son Jesus Christ, be all glory, honour, might and majesty, for ever and ever. Our greetings to all the people of God. Our companions here send their greetings – and so, with all his family, does

Your scribe,
Evarestus [26]

21. It was the second day of the first fortnight of Xanthicus, seven days before the kalends of March, when our blessed Polycarp died his martyr's death two hours after midday on the Greater Sabbath.[27] The official responsible for his arrest was Herod; the High Priest was Philip of Tralles; and the proconsul was Statius Quadratus – but the ruling monarch was Jesus Christ,[28] who reigns for ever and ever. To him be ascribed all glory, honour, majesty, and an eternal throne from generation to generation. Amen.

22. And now, brethren, we bid you farewell. Order your lives by the word of the Gospel of Jesus Christ (with whom be

glory to God the Father and the Holy Spirit) for the salvation of His holy elect; even as did Polycarp the Blessed in his martyrdom. May it be our lot to be found following in his footsteps in the kingdom of Jesus Christ.

COPYISTS' NOTES

(i) The above account has been transcribed by Gaius from the papers of his contemporary Irenaeus, who was a disciple of Polycarp. I, Socrates, have now made this copy here in Corinth from Gaius' manuscripts. Grace be with you all.

(ii) I, Pionius,[29] have made a fresh transcript of those earlier writings. I found them after Polycarp the Blessed had revealed their whereabouts in a vision, as I will explain hereafter. Time had reduced them almost to tatters, but I gathered them carefully together, in the hope that the Lord Jesus Christ may likewise gather myself amongst His elect into His heavenly kingdom. To Him, with the Father and the Holy Ghost, be glory for ever and ever. Amen.

NOTES

1. See note 1 on Clement's *First Epistle to the Corinthians*.
2. A town in Phrygia, on the highway to Cappadocia. No other mention of it has been found in the writings of the time.
3. i.e. the Passion of Christ. Throughout the story the narrator takes pains to indicate the resemblances between Polycarp's sufferings and those of his Master.
4. The Proconsul of Asia (the richest of the Roman provinces) occupied a post hardly inferior in state to that of a Victorian Viceroy of India. It was the blue ribbon of a professional career, and was held at this time by Lucius Statius Quadratus.
5. The infidels (lit. 'atheists'). This epithet was as commonly applied to Christians by the heathen of Polycarp's day as it was by the Barbary corsairs of a later age.
6. Cowardice was supposed to be a Phrygian failing. Tertullian,

De Anim: xx, says, 'the writers of comedies make jokes about the faint-heartedness of the Phrygians'.

7. The impulsive self-surrender of Quintus did him no credit, since it was not in the spirit of such Gospel precepts as *When they persecute you in this city, flee ye into another (Matthew* x, 23). In contrast Polycarp, as we shall see in a moment, acted in accordance with these, and made no attempt to anticipate his arrest.

8. Since the betrayers were said to be 'of his own household', and since we find him in the next chapter ordering his captors to be supplied with food and drink, it seems probable that this farm was Polycarp's own property. This would agree with the tradition that he was a man of substance.

9. Literally, the *Eirenarch*, or Peace-Keeper. He was a personage of distinction, somewhat similar to our High Sheriff. His office was one of the public services that were undertaken by prominent citizens at their own cost.

10. A parallel with the Passion is suggested. *Are ye come out as against a thief, with swords and staves for to take me? (Matthew* xxvi, 55.)

11. Recalling Christ's entry into Jerusalem on Palm Sunday.

12. Presumably a sabbath which coincided with one of the Jewish festivals; as with us, for example, All Saints Day will sometimes fall on a Sunday.

13. The divine title 'Lord' could not in conscience be applied by Christians to a mortal. The offering of incense 'and so forth' was part of the customary ritual of emperor-worship.

14. Namely the goddess Fortune. The originator of this oath was Julius Caesar, who believed himself to be a special favourite of hers; but in later times it became an official formula. Since it implied recognition of a heathen deity, it was obviously unacceptable to Christians.

15. The narrator means us to catch an echo here of the similar reluctance of Pilate to condemn Jesus.

16. Perhaps said sarcastically, or possibly in a genuine hope that Polycarp might be able to evoke a popular demonstration in his favour, and so justify his release.

17. To facillitate local government under the Empire the principal cities of each province were formed into joint associations for civil and religious purposes. The best known of these was the Asian Confederation (the *commune Asiae*), and its president, the Asiarch, was the leading figure in the province after the Proconsul. His

chief duties were the superintendence of the emperor-worship throughout the province (on which account he is referred to by his official title of High Priest in chapter 21), and the presidency of the games and festivals which were held in the federated cities. The expenses of the office were considerable, as he was expected to bear much of the cost of these games; and it is significant that, as we learn below (ch. 21), the present Asiarch, Philip, was a citizen of the wealthy city of Tralles.

18. The beast-fights were only one item in a programme which might also include chariot races, athletic contests of all kinds, gladiatorial combats, sham battles, and other performances. The wild animals fought either with each other or with men; the latter being sometimes condemned criminals, or sometimes trained professionals like the modern Spanish bull-fighters.

19. This pathetic detail suggests that the exertion was now too much for the old man, who usually depended on friends or disciples for such small services.

20. The narrator uses the Roman word *confector* here, meaning literally 'a finisher-off'. They were employed in the circus to give the *coup de grâce* to wounded animals or men. As the beast-fights had only recently ended, this man would still be within call, though executions by fire were ordinarily none of his business.

21. The emblem of a departing Christian soul. (But this may be a later addition to the text; Eusebius says nothing of it.)

22. Had the body fetched out publicly (literally 'placed it in the midst'). 'Withdrew it from private ownership; confiscated the body in the name of the State' (Kleist).

23. For security reasons the place is not named.

24. Here for the first time we find the idea, afterwards so familiar, that the day of a saint's death is reckoned as his 'birthday'.

25. Nothing is known of him – unless he may be the 'Marcian' (*sic*) to whom Eusebius says that one of the treatises of Irenaeus was dedicated (*H.E.* v, 26; Penguin edition, p. 234).

26. The (unknown) scribe who has written out Marcion's composition.

27. For the problems of the date of the martyrdom, see the Preface to this epistle.

28. A deliberate substitution for the name of the heathen emperor Antoninus Pius, which would normally complete this kind of chronological note.

29. Pionius was the fourth-century author of a fabulous life of Polycarp, in which he incorporates the whole of the *Martyrdom*. The promised account of his vision presumably appeared in a later portion of the work, but this has not survived.

*

THE EPISTLE
TO
DIOGNETUS

*

The Epistle to Diognetus

The anonymous *Epistle to Diognetus* – which is a treatise rather than a letter – purports to be the reply to an inquiring heathen's desire for information about the beliefs and customs of Christians. 'Why', he is supposed to have asked, 'do they hold the cults of both Greeks and Jews in equal aversion? What is the real nature of their own religion? Why has it only recently made its appearance in the world?' In answer to these questions the author, after an exposition of the follies of Greek idol-worship and a castigation of Jewish superstitions, contrasts the supernatural nature of the Christian revelation with the man-made rites of its rivals, and then proceeds to draw a singularly beautiful picture of the manner of life practised in the Christian communities of his day. The identity of Diognetus himself, apparently a pagan of high rank, is unknown. There is a Diognetus among the many personages to whom the emperor Marcus Aurelius, in his *Meditations*, has recorded his gratitude; and some critics, including Lightfoot, have been inclined to think that he was the recipient of the epistle. The more recent theory of Dom P. Andriessen, however, would identify Diognetus with the earlier emperor Hadrian; for Andriessen has argued strongly that this epistle is in reality the supposedly lost *Apology* of Quadratus,* a defence of Christianity known to have been addressed to Hadrian in the tenth year of his reign. (Diognetus, which means 'Heaven-born', may well have been one of the honorific titles of the emperor.) If Andriessen's views are accepted, we must date the epistle somewhere about 124; a period with which the writer's description of contemporary Church life, as well as the simplicity of his theology, is perfectly consistent.

It is only by the most improbable good fortune that the epistle has come to our knowledge at all. Strangely enough, no mention of it or quotation from it has been found anywhere in the

---

* An early Father who passed the first part of his life in Asia Minor and afterwards became a bishop of the Church at Athens.

rest of patristic literature. Furthermore, the only text of it existed in a single manuscript until as late as the sixteenth century, when three copies of it were made.* This one original manuscript later perished in the flames of Strassburg during the Franco-German war of 1870; but happily the copies had been carefully collated with it only a short time before. There are gaps in the text in chapters 7 and 10, and at the end of the tenth chapter the epistle breaks off abruptly. The remaining two chapters, which are by a quite different hand, appear to form part of a sermon intended for delivery on the feast of the Epiphany (or possibly Easter). The style of their composition has led many critics to ascribe them to the third-century presbyter Hippolytus of Rome.

* It was a collection of treatises by Justin Martyr, with the epistle to Diognetus appended. In consequence the authorship of the epistle was for long erroneously attributed to Justin.

1. I have noticed, my lord Diognetus, the deep interest you have been showing in Christianity, and the close and careful inquiries you have been making about it. You would like to know what God Christians believe in, and what sort of cult they practise which enables them to set so little store by this world, and even to make light of death itself – since they reject the deities revered by the Greeks no less than they disclaim the superstitions professed by the Jews. You are curious, too, about the warm fraternal affection they all feel for one another. Also, you are puzzled as to why this new breed of men, or at least this novel manner of life, has only come into our lives recently, instead of much earlier.

I salute this eagerness for knowledge on your part; and I pray God, the Author of both speech and hearing, to grant me such use of my tongue that you may derive the fullest benefit from listening to me, and to you such use of your ears that I may have no cause to regret having spoken.

THE FOLLIES OF PAGANISM

2. Begin, then, by clearing your mind[1] of the prejudices it harbours. Shake off the hidebound notions which can only lead to error, and put yourself in the position of a brand-new man on the point of hearing what you yourself admit to be a brand-new language.

Then take a good look – with your intelligence, not just with your eyes – at the forms and substances of those objects which you call gods and hold to be divine. Is this one here, for instance, anything other than a block of stone, identical in kind with the flags we tread under our feet? Is not that one there made out of brass, of no finer quality than the common utensils that are manufactured for our everyday use? A third of wood, already rotting into decay? A fourth of silver, needing someone to keep an eye on it all the time for fear of thieves? A fifth of iron, pitted all over with rust, and a sixth of no better-looking earthenware than the articles they turn out for the humblest domestic purposes? Is not every single one of these made of materials that are perishable? Was one not made by a stone-cutter, another by a brassfounder, a third by a silversmith, a fourth by a potter? And up to the moment when the skill of those craftsmen gave them their present forms, was it not just as practicable – indeed, is it not just as practicable even now – for every one of them to have been made into something quite different? Moreover, supposing that ordinary pots and pans of similar material were to be put into the hands of those crafts-men, could they not be turned into gods like these? – or, contrariwise, could not the images you adore be perfectly well re-fashioned by human hands into commonplace pots and pans like any others? In a word, are they not, one and all, nothing but dumb, blind, lifeless things, without sense, without movement, rotting and decaying?

Do you really call these things gods, and really do service to them? Yes, indeed you do; you worship them – and you end up by becoming like them. Is it not because we Christians refuse to acknowledge their divinity that you dislike us so? All the same, there is in fact very little reverence in the way you treat them, even while you imagine and believe that you are glorifying them. It is surely a mockery and an affront to them that, so long as these venerated deities are only made of stone or pottery, you leave them quite unprotected, but when they are silver or gold, then you lock them up every night, and post watchmen over them all day, in case they might be stolen. And if they are really endowed with sense, the sort of honours you pay to them must be more of a humiliation than a tribute; and if they are not, then you are making nonsense of them when you adore them with the blood and fat of your sacrifices. Imagine one of your-selves putting up with that kind of thing, or allowing it to be done to him! No human being would tolerate such indignity, because he possesses sense and reason; the stone only puts up with it because it has none. So your own actions establish its insensibility.

There is plenty more I could say about the refusal of Christians to make themselves thralls to gods of this sort; but if the above considerations are not enough for anybody, I see no point in pursuing the subject further.

THE FOLLIES OF JUDAISM

3. Next, I expect what you most want to hear about is our Christian unwillingness to accept the faith of the Jews. Admittedly, since they will have no truck with the sort of religion I have just been describing, Jews may fairly claim to be devotees of the one true God, and to acknowledge Him as their Sovereign. Nevertheless, in so far as they do Him service with rites similar to those of the heathen, they are in error. For if the Greeks must stand convicted of absurdity by the offerings they make to senseless and dumb idols, the Jews ought to realize that it shows equal absurdity, and no true piety, to conceive of God Himself as in want of such things. The Maker of heaven and earth and all therein, the Supplier of our every need, could never Himself be in any need of the very things which are actually His own gifts to the self-styled givers. Indeed, so long as they believe themselves to be fulfilling their sacrificial duty to Him by means of blood and fat and burnt-offerings, and fancy they are doing Him honour by such rites, I cannot see that there is anything to choose between them and the men who lavish similar attentions on deaf and dumb idols. One party, it seems, makes its offerings to creatures which cannot partake of the gifts, and the other to One who needs none of them.

4. As for their scrupulousness about meats, and their superstitions about the sabbath,[2] and their much-vaunted circumcision, and their pretentious festivals and new-moon-observances – all of them too nonsensical to be worth discussing – I hardly think you need instruction from me. For how can it be anything but impious to accept some of the things which God has created for our use and assert their creation to have been commendable, but to reject others as being needless and good-for-nothing? And what can there be but profanity in the slanderous charge that God

objects to a good deed being done on a sabbath day? And surely, when they boast that a bodily mutilation is evidence of their inclusion among the elect, as though it gave them some special claim on God's love, what does this deserve but to be laughed out of court? As for the minute way they scrutinize the moon and stars[3] for the purpose of ritually commemorating months and days, and chop up the divinely appointed cycle of the seasons to suit their own fancies, pronouncing some to be times for feasting and others for mourning – could anyone pretend that this indicates true reverence, and not simply a deranged intellect?

I imagine you have heard enough now to see how right the Christians are in repudiating the folly and delusion common to these two cults, as well as the fussy practices of which the Jews are so proud. At the same time, however, you must never expect to learn the inward mystery of their own religion from merely human lips.

CHARACTERISTICS OF THE
CHRISTIAN COMMUNITY

5. The difference between Christians and the rest of mankind is not a matter of nationality, or language, or customs. Christians do not live apart in separate cities of their own, speak any special dialect, nor practise any eccentric way of life. The doctrine they profess is not the invention of busy human minds and brains, nor are they, like some, adherents of this or that school of human thought. They pass their lives in whatever township – Greek or foreign – each man's lot has determined; and conform to ordinary local usage in their clothing, diet, and other habits. Nevertheless, the organization of their community does exhibit some features that are remarkable, and even surprising. For instance, though they are residents at home in their own countries, their behaviour there is more like that of transients;[4] they take their full part as citizens, but they also submit to anything and everything as if they were aliens.[5] For them, any foreign country is a motherland, and any motherland is a foreign coun-

try. Like other men, they marry and beget children, though
they do not expose their infants. Any Christian is free to share
his neighbour's table, but never his marriage-bed.[6] Though
destiny has placed them here in the flesh, they do not live after
the flesh; their days are passed on the earth, but their citizenship is above in the heavens. They obey the prescribed laws, but
in their own private lives they transcend the laws. They show
love to all men – and all men persecute them. They are mis-
understood, and condemned;[7] yet by suffering death they are
quickened into life. They are poor, yet making many rich; lack-
ing all things, yet having all things in abundance. They are dis-
honoured, yet made glorious in their very dishonour; slandered,
yet vindicated. They repay calumny with blessings, and abuse
with courtesy. For the good they do, they suffer stripes as evil-
doers; and under the strokes they rejoice like men given new life.
Jews assail them as heretics, and Greeks harass them with persecutions; and yet of all their ill-wishers there is not one who can
produce good grounds for his hostility.

6. To put it briefly, the relation of Christians to the world is
that of a soul to the body. As the soul is diffused through every
part of the body, so are Christians through all the cities of the
world. The soul, too, inhabits the body, while at the same time
forming no part of it; and Christians inhabit the world, but they
are not part of the world. The soul, invisible herself, is immured
within a visible body; so Christians can be recognized in the
world, but their Christianity itself remains hidden from the eye.
The flesh hates the soul, and wars against her without any
provocation, because she is an obstacle to its own self-indulgence;
and the world similarly hates the Christians without provocation, because they are opposed to its pleasures. All the same, the
soul loves the flesh and all its members, despite their hatred for
her; and Christians, too, love those who hate them. The soul,
shut up inside the body, nevertheless holds the body together;
and though they are confined within the world as in a dungeon,
it is Christians who hold the world together. The soul, which is
immortal, must dwell in a mortal tabernacle; and Christians, as
they sojourn for a while in the midst of corruptibility here, look

for incorruptibility in the heavens. Finally, just as to be stinted of food and drink makes for the soul's improvement, so when Christians are every day subjected to ill-treatment, they increase the more in numbers. Such is the high post of duty in which God has placed them, and it is their moral duty not to shrink from it.

7. For, as I said before, it is not an earthly discovery that has been entrusted to them. The thing they guard so jealously is no product of mortal thinking, and what has been committed to them is the stewardship of no human mysteries. The Almighty Himself, the Creator of the universe, the God whom no eye can discern, has sent down His very own Truth from heaven, His own holy and incomprehensible Word, to plant it among men and ground it in their hearts. To this end He has not, as one might imagine, sent to mankind some servant of His, some angel or prince; it is none of the great ones of the earth, nor even one of the vice-gerents of heaven. It is no other than the universal Artificer and Constructor Himself, by whose agency God made the heavens and set the seas their bounds;[8] whose mystic word the elements of creation submissively obey; by whom the sun is assigned the limits of his course by day, and at whose command by night the obedient moon unveils her beams, and each compliant star follows circling in her train. Ordainer, Disposer, and Ruler of all things is he; of heaven and all that heaven holds, of earth and all that is in earth, of sea and every creature therein; of fires, ether, and bottomless pit; of things above, and things below, and things in the midst. Such was the Messenger God sent to men.

And was his coming, as a man might suppose, in power, in terror, and in dread? Not so; it was in gentleness and humility. As a king sending his royal son, so sent He him; as God He sent him; as Man to men He sent him; and that because He was fain to save us by persuasion, and not by compulsion – for there is no compulsion found with God. His mission was no pursuit or hounding of us, it was an invitation to us; it was in love, not in judgement that He sent him (though one day He will indeed send him to judge us, and then who shall abide the day of his coming?).

... [Have you not seen Christians]* flung to the wild beasts to make them deny their Lord, and yet remaining undefeated? Do you not see how the more of them suffer such punishments, the larger grows the number of the rest? These things do not look like the work of man; they are the power of God, and the evident tokens of His presence.

THE MYSTERY OF THE INCARNATION

8. Before his advent, who among mankind had any notion at all of what God is? Or do you accept the vapid and ludicrous suggestions of your own pretentious philosophers? – some of whom assure us that God is Fire[9] (thus giving the name of God to what they will surely come to one day themselves!), some that He is Water, and others one of the other various elements of His creation. If any of those ideas were admissible, there would be no reason why anything else in the world could not be declared to be God. Assertions of that sort are no more than the hocus-pocus, the 'hey, presto!', of professional illusionists, for no man living has ever seen Him or known Him; it is He Himself who has given us the revelation of Himself. But He has only revealed Himself to faith, by which alone are we permitted to know God. For God, though Lord and Architect of the whole world, who made and set in order each single thing that is, was something more than loving towards mankind, He was long-suffering as well. (So He has always been, and is still, and ever shall be: merciful, kind, slow to anger, and true; there is none so good as He.) He conceived a design, great and beyond all telling, and He imparted it to none

* There is a gap in the manuscript here, where some such phrase must be supplied.

but His Son alone. (And so long as He maintained this secrecy, and kept His own wise counsel, it seemed as though He had no care for us and had put us out of His mind; but as soon as He disclosed it, through His beloved Son, and revealed what had been planned since the beginning, then straightway He poured out all the fullness of His bounty upon us, permitting us to share His benefactions and to see and know such blessings as none of us could ever have looked for.)

9. Next, after making these dispositions in His mind with the Son, He left us to live for the meanwhile as we pleased, giving free rein to our unruly instincts and being at the mercy of sensuality and lust. This was not because He took any pleasure in those sins of ours; all He was doing was to put up with them. It was not that He was sanctioning that former era of lawlessness; rather, He was preparing this present era of righteousness, to the intent that we, who in those days had been proved by our own works unworthy to achieve life, might in these days be made worthy of it by the goodness of God – and that, after clearly showing our inability to enter into the kingdom of God by our own power, we might now by God's power be made able. Accordingly, when our iniquity had come to its full height, and it was clear beyond all mistaking that retribution in the form of punishment and death must be looked for, the hour arrived in which God had determined to make known from then onwards His loving-kindness and His power. How surpassing is the love and tenderness of God! In that hour, instead of hating us and rejecting us and remembering our wickednesses against us, He showed how long-suffering He is. He bore with us, and in pity He took our sins upon Himself and gave His own Son as a ransom for us – the Holy for the wicked, the Sinless for sinners, the Just for the unjust, the Incorrupt for the corrupt, the Immortal for the mortal. For was there, indeed, anything except His righteousness that could have availed to cover our sins? In whom could we, in our lawlessness and ungodliness, have been made holy, but in the Son of God alone? O sweet exchange! O unsearchable working! O benefits unhoped for! – that the wickedness of multitudes should thus be hidden in the One

holy, and the holiness of One should sanctify the countless wicked!

In times past, He convinced us that our human nature by itself lacked the power of attaining to life; today, He reveals to us a Saviour who has power to save even the powerless. The purpose behind both of these acts is that we should believe in His goodness, and should look on Him as our Nourisher, Father, Teacher, Counsellor, Healer, Wisdom, Light, Honour, Glory, Power, and Life, and have no anxiety about our clothing or our food.

PRACTICAL CONCLUSIONS

10. Now, if you too desire to have this faith, knowledge of the Father must be your first lesson.

God loved the race of men. It was for their sakes that He made the world; it was to them that He gave dominion over everything in it. On them He bestowed reason and understanding, and they alone received permission to lift up their eyes to Him. He formed them in His own image; He sent His only-begotten Son to them; He promised them the kingdom of heaven, and to those who have loved Him He will surely give it.

Once you have grasped these truths, think how your joy will overflow, and what love you will feel for Him who loved you so. And if you love Him, you will become an imitator of His goodness. Do not be surprised that a man should be an imitator of God; he can, since God has willed it so. But happiness is not to be found in dominating one's fellows, or in wanting to have more than his weaker brethren, or in possessing riches and riding rough-shod over his inferiors. No one can become an imitator of God like that, for such things are wholly alien to His greatness. But if a man will shoulder his neighbour's burden; if he be ready to supply another's need from his own abundance; if, by sharing the blessings he has received from God with those who are in want, he himself becomes a god to those who receive his bounty – such a man is indeed an imitator of God. And then you will see, as you walk the earth, that there is a God who is operative in heaven; then you will begin to dilate on His mysteries; and you will know love and admiration for those who incur persecution by their refusal to deny Him. Then, too, you will see through the deceitfulness and error of this world, once you have found what it is to live the true life of heaven, and have learnt to despise the seeming death of the body and to dread only the real death which is reserved for those condemned to the fires of eternity – fires that will torment their victims for evermore. In the knowledge of those fires, your admiration will go out to all who endure a more transient flame for righteousness' sake, and you will call them blessed indeed.

PART 2. THE HOMILY

11. I am not talking of anything novel or strange, or raising any new questions. Although I am an instructor of the Gentiles now, I was a pupil of the Apostles once; and what was delivered to me then, I now minister faithfully to students of the truth. How can anyone, who has been rightly taught and learnt to love the Word, not wish to be told the precise nature of the revelations which that Word so openly made to His disciples? Visibly present among them, the Word made His disclosures to them in the plainest of language; though unrecognized by the unbelieving, He discoursed without reserve to the disciples; and because they were reckoned faithful by Him, they came to know the mysteries of God. That was the purpose for which God sent the Word to be manifested to the world. He was despised by the Chosen People, but preached by the Apostles and believed in by the Gentiles. Though He has existed since the beginning, He came as one appearing newly; though we know Him to be from old, He is born ever anew in the hearts of His saints. This is He who is from everlasting, this is He who is accounted this day a Son. Through Him the church is enriched; abounding grace is multiplied among the saints, furnishing understanding, revealing mysteries,[10] proclaiming times and seasons,[11] and rejoicing over the faithful believers – the grace which is granted to every

seeker who does not violate his vows of faith, or transgress the
bounds fixed by the Fathers. And then –

> A chant celebrates the fear of the Law,
> The grace of the Prophets is made known,
> The faith of the Gospels is implanted,
> The tradition of the Apostles is secured,
> and
> The grace of the Church waxes jubilant.[12]

Grieve not this grace,[13] and then you shall understand the
things which the Word, when it is His will to do so, imparts
through the lips of those he chooses. For whatsoever that com-
manding will of the Word impels us to utter, we are at pains
to communicate to you, in our love for the truths He has revealed to us.

12. Once these truths have been brought before you, and you
have listened heedfully to them, you will know what God
bestows on those who rightly love Him. They become a very
paradise of delight; they make a grove to spring up and flourish
within themselves, which yields all manner of nourishment and
adorns them with fruits of every kind. For in that garden are
planted both the Tree of Knowledge and the Tree of Life – for
it is not the Tree of Knowledge that causes death; the deadly
thing is disobedience. Scripture clearly says, *In the beginning
God planted in the midst of the garden the tree of knowledge
and the tree of life*; thereby showing that the way to life lies
through knowledge. It is only because the first-created couple
used it improperly that, through the wiles of the serpent, they
were stripped of all they had. Without knowledge there can be
no life,[14] and without life there can be no trustworthy knowledge; which is why the two trees were planted side by side. The
Apostle saw the force of this when he told us, *knowledge
makes a windbag, but love is a builder*; that was his rebuke to
the knowledge which is exercised without regard to the life-
giving precepts of the truth. For a man who claims to know, but
is without the knowledge which is real and attested by life,
knows nothing; the serpent has tricked him, because his heart is

not set on life. But he who possesses knowledge coupled with fear, and whose quest for life is earnest, may plant in hope and look for fruit.

Let the heart of you, then, be knowledge, and let your life be true inward reception of the Word. Tending your tree in this way, and gathering its fruits, you will at all times enjoy a harvest that is pleasing to God, and one which no serpent can touch and no deceit penetrate. No longer then is Eve seduced; trust is placed in a Virgin; salvation is proclaimed; missioners are endowed with understanding; the Lord's Passover goes forward; the seasons are brought together and fittingly set in order; the Word rejoices to instruct the saints; and through Him God is glorified.

To Him be glory for ever and ever. Amen.

NOTES

1. Literally 'purify yourself'. Purification was required of anyone about to receive initiation into the mysteries, and Diognetus is here regarded as being in that position.

2. 'That on which of all else the Pharisees laid most stress was the observance of the sabbath. On no other subject is Rabbinical teaching more painfully minute, and more manifestly incongruous to its professed object.' (Edersheim, *The Life and Times of Jesus the Messiah.*)

3. Since the Hebrew year was lunar, not solar, the correct determination of each new moon was essential for the fixing of the various annual festivals. This was not ascertained by astronomical calculation, but by direct ocular evidence; for which purpose the Sanhedrin used to meet in session and hear testimony from as many trustworthy witnesses as possible that they had seen a new moon. The month was then authoritatively declared to have begun, and beacon fires on the hilltops immediately flashed the tidings to the furthest boundaries of the land.

4. Transients, or 'resident aliens'. See note 1 on the Inscription of Clement's Epistle, where the same Greek word is applied to the Corinthian church. It became a favourite description of the Christian community in any locality, and has eventually made its way into the English language as 'parish'.

THE EPISTLE TO DIOGNETUS

5. As meekly as the foreign residents of a city put up with all kinds of restrictions and impositions, so the Christian inhabitants accept the insults and indignities to which their religion exposes them.

6. So Tertullian: 'everything is in common with us, except our wives' (*Apol.* xxxix, 11).

7. Popular ignorance of the real religion of Christians results in slanderous misrepresentations of their beliefs, on the strength of which they are often sentenced to death.

8. Cf. *Hebrews* i, 2: 'his son, whom he hath appointed heir of all things, by whom also he made the world'.

9. Heraclitus of Ephesus (*fl.* 513 B.C.) had declared fire to be the fundamental source of everything in the universe, and this afterwards became the accepted doctrine of the Stoic philosophers. Earlier Thales of Miletus had taught that this *prima materia* was water, and his successor Anaximenes that it was air.

10. This quasi-personification of Grace as an active agent makes it virtually synonymous here with the Holy Spirit.

11. The fasts and festivals of the Christian Church are not determined by natural phenomena, as were those of the Jews (ch. 4), but by the guidance of the Holy Spirit.

12. It is tempting to see in these lines a glimpse of the early Church's worship, with psalms, Bible-reading, and a sermon.

13. A deliberate echo of St Paul's 'Grieve not the Holy Spirit of God' (*Ephesians* iv, 30).

14. The writer would have no patience with the modern demand for 'religion without dogma'. God, it is often forgotten, is not only to be loved 'with all thy heart', but also 'with all thy mind'.

*

THE EPISTLE
OF BARNABAS

*

The Epistle of Barnabas

A problem which caused the early Church much perplexity was the relation of Christianity to Judaism: the new and the old inheritors of the same Divine covenant. This is the theme of the unknown writer to whom we owe the so-called *Epistle of Barnabas*. His own answer to the question is a direct and uncompromising one; he denies flatly that there is any historical link at all between Judaism and the Gospel. All the rites and ceremonies of the Law, he tells us, had been intended by God simply as mystical pointers to Christ; but the Jewish people had been seduced by an evil angel into a literal instead of a spiritual understanding of them, leading them to regard the observance of these ordinances as a sufficient end in itself. It is true that the insight of a few righteous men – Moses, David, and the prophets – had divined the true meaning of the Law; but Israel in general had failed to understand it aright, and consequently all claim to possess the Covenant had been taken away from them and reserved instead for the Christians. He exposes this alleged misconception of the Old Testament in an elaborate series of allegorical interpretations, purporting to show how in every case the ancient Hebrew institutions prefigured their spiritual counterparts in the Christian dispensation, and how the Cross of Christ had been foreshadowed from the beginning under a variety of types.

Nothing is known of the identity of the author, and the epistle itself gives us no clue. In ancient times it was held by many to be the work of the Apostle Barnabas. Clement of Alexandria, for instance, who quotes largely from it, expressly ascribes it to 'him who preached in company with Paul',[*] and Jerome to 'Barnabas the Cypriot, ordained an apostle to the Gentiles along with Paul'.[†] On the other hand, Eusebius includes it among the writings which were not generally regarded at inspired;[‡]

[*] *Strom.* ii, 6.
[†] *De Viris Illustr:* vi. [‡] *H.E.* iii, 25 (Penguin edition, p. 134).

and it is improbable that this stigma would have been attached to it if it had been widely believed to be of apostolic origin. The evidence of the epistle itself, moreover, is decisively against the authorship of Barnabas. To take only one consideration, it is impossible that he, who was a Levite, and had even been criticized by St Paul for his too great attachment to the Jewish party,* could have been capable of attributing the Law of Moses to the wiles of a demon. The writer, whoever he was, may indeed have been named Barnabas; but his style, and his allegorical method of interpreting Scripture, suggest that, like Apollos, he was most probably 'a learned Jew of Alexandria' who had been converted to Christianity.

The date of the epistle can be narrowed down with reasonable certainty to within sixty years. Since it mentions the destruction of Jerusalem, which took place in the year A.D.70, it cannot have been written before that year. But it makes no reference to the revolt of Bar-Cocheba in 132, when Jerusalem was devastated by the Romans for the second time; and as it is hardly conceivable that the writer, had he known of it, would have ignored an event so apt to his purpose, we must assume that his letter was already in existence before this time. Recent critics, indeed, have suggested an even closer approximation to the date. It is known that before the outbreak of Bar-Cocheba's rebellion the emperor Hadrian had been inclined to reverse the harsh policy of his predecessor Trajan towards the Jews and to treat them with a new leniency. It is easy to believe that this would lead to a prompt revival of their national aspirations and a vigorous resurgence of proselytizing, which might well have tended to shake the new-found allegiance of some of their brethren to Christianity. In such circumstances, if the situation had seemed to our author to call urgently for a counter-offensive, his epistle would have been issued round about the year 130; and this, in fact, is the date now preferred by most scholars.

Until the nineteenth century our knowledge of the *Epistle of Barnabas* was limited to a Latin version of the first seventeen chapters. But in 1859 the discovery of the Codex Sinaiticus

* *Galatians* ii, 13.

190

revealed for the first time the Greek text of the letter in its entirety. Together with the *Shepherd* of Hermas and the *Didache*, it had been added as a kind of appendix to the books of the New Testament, as though to indicate the quasi-scriptural authority of these writings. Nevertheless, it is possible that the seventeen chapters of the Latin version may have represented the original form of the epistle, since the writer's treatise against Judaism comes to an end with the last of them. The portion found in the Greek manuscript at once enters upon a completely new theme, introduced by the words, *Now let us pass on to quite a different sort of instruction*; after which we are presented with a series of moral precepts for the Christian life, largely transcribed from the Two Ways of the *Didache*. This second portion, which has so little apparent connexion with the first, may perhaps have been added by another hand a generation or so later.

The ordinary reader may find himself puzzled by the seeming inaccuracy of many of Barnabas's profuse quotations from Scripture. There are three factors, any of which – either by itself or in combination with others – may account for this. In the first place, it must not be forgotten that Barnabas is using the only Bible that was familiar to the Greek-speaking world, the Greek (LXX, or Septuagint) translation of the original Hebrew books. Secondly, his standards of exactitude are not high; he often quotes from a not very reliable memory, and is content to give the general sense of a text instead of its exact words. And finally, it must be confessed that he has regrettably few scruples about altering or adding to a Scriptural text to strengthen his argument. The result of all this is that his quotations sometimes become almost unrecognizable when they are compared with the original sources.

How much interest a modern reader finds in the tract will depend to a great extent upon his attitude to the mystical interpretation of Scripture. He may be fascinated by the author's ingenuity in detecting or inventing an esoteric significance in the Old Testament ordinances, or on the other hand he may be repelled by such extravagant allegorization. It must be remembered, though, that however far the practice may have fallen out of fashion today, it was universally esteemed in ancient times; and in principal it has undeniably the warrant of the New Testament writers. (The *Epistle to the Hebrews* is a notable example.) What is certain is that the early Church, at all events, held the *Epistle of Barnabas* in the highest regard, and reckoned it as only coming short of the authority of Holy Scripture itself.

The Epistle of Barnabas

*Greetings to you, my sons and my
daughters. In the name of the Lord
who loved us, peace.*

1. Rich and eminent indeed are the evidences of holiness with
which God has endowed you; and such a root has His gift of
spiritual grace taken in your hearts, that I am overjoyed by the
bliss and glory of your souls. It deepens the happiness of my
own hopes of salvation, when I see such an outpouring of the
Spirit upon you from the riches of the Divine fountainhead.
After longing so much for a sight of you, the reality has left me
overwhelmed.

One thing at least I know, and am deeply conscious of in my
own mind. Since I last spoke to you, there is a great deal that I
have come to understand; for on my pilgrimage towards holiness
I have had the companionship of the Lord. Consequently I too,
like Him, am bound to think of you as dearer to me than life
itself, because of the intense faith and love that have their dwelling in your hearts, as you hope for that life which is His. Also,
I have a feeling that if my care on your behalf prompts me to
pass on some part of what I myself have received, it may earn
me a reward for being of service to souls of such merit. For these
reasons I have been at pains to send you this small treatise; by
which, in addition to your faith, you may be put in complete
possession of knowledge as well.

The divine principles are three in number. Faith begins and
ends with Hope, hope of life; judgement begins and ends with
Holiness; and the works of holiness are evidenced by Love, and
the joy and gladness it brings.

Moreover, through the prophets the Master has laid open to
us both past and present history, and has even given us an
anticipatory taste of the future as well. It follows that when we
see events coming to pass step by step precisely as He told us,

this ought to enrich and heighten the reverential fear we pay to Him. So what I propose to do – not as a teacher, but as one of yourselves – is to put a few thoughts before you that should bring comfort to your hearts in the situation we are now facing.[1]

2. For these are evil days, with the Worker of Evil himself in the ascendant; and this means that we must apply ourselves to a careful study of the Divine ordinances, having patience and the fear of God to reinforce our faith, and resignation and self-discipline for allies. Provided we keep a firm hold on these, in a spirit of holiness, in all matters that have to do with the Lord, then wisdom, intelligence, understanding, and enlightenment will gladly come to keep them company.

OF SACRIFICES

Now, what the Lord has made abundantly clear to us, by the mouths of all His prophets, is that sacrifices, burnt-offerings and oblations are things of which He has not the smallest need. His own words are: *What do I care about all these sacrifices of yours, says the Lord. I am satiated with burnt-offerings; I want neither fat of lambs, blood of bulls or goats, nor your own attendance here in my sight. Never again are you to come trampling my courts; it is useless to proffer me gifts of fine flour; incense is detestable to me, and I cannot endure your new moons and your sabbaths.** All these things He swept away; intending the New Law of our Lord Jesus Christ to impose no yoke of coercion, and its Oblation to be no offering of human hands. And in another place He says to them, *When your fathers came out of the land of Egypt, did I ever tell them to offer me burnt-offerings and sacrifices?†* *Never; all I told them was, None of you is to harbour an evil thought in his heart against a neighbour, or any tenderness for broken vows.‡* Now, unless we are altogether without understanding, we ought surely to detect our Father's kindly purpose for ourselves in this. For it is to us that

* *Isaiah* i, 11–13.   † *Jeremiah* vii, 22.   ‡ *Zechariah* viii, 17.

He is speaking here, in His desire that we should discover the right way of approaching Him, instead of going astray as they did. And what He tells us is, *the sacrifice for the Lord is a contrite heart;* a heart that glorifies its Maker is a sweet savour to the Lord.†* It behoves us, my brothers, to inquire very closely into this matter of our salvation; for fear the Evil One should insinuate his wicked wiles into our hearts, and manage to cast us out from the life that lies before us.

OF FASTING

3. In this connexion He also says to them, *Why are you keeping a fast, so that my ears are being assailed this day with the whining of your voices? This is no fast of my appointing, says the Lord; not this humiliating of a man's soul. You may twist your necks into hoops and wear sackcloth and put down ashes to lie on, but you shall not call that an acceptable fast.* And then, addressing ourselves, He goes on, *Look, the fast of my choice is this: relax all your iniquitous restrictions, loosen the shackles of your oppressive covenants, let your ruined debtors go free, and tear up all your unjust agreements. Break up your bread into portions for the starving; and if you see a man who is in want of clothing, fit him out yourself. Bring in the homeless under your own roof; and should you happen to catch sight of some person of low degree, be sure that neither you nor anyone belonging to you casts an eye of scorn upon him. Then shall your light shine out like the rising sun; healing shall dawn swiftly upon you, and you will march forward with holiness as your vanguard and the glory of God on either flank. Then God will hear you when you call, and while the words are still on your lips he will say, Look, here I am – if only you will forswear imprisonings and violence, leave off your resentful murmurings, give your bread to the hungry with a good grace, and have pity on the soul that is afflicted.‡*

Thus, my brothers, patiently looking ahead to the day when a people prepared in His Beloved should hold the faith in its per-

* *Psalm* li, 17.   † Source lost.   ‡ *Isaiah* lviii, 5ff.

fect purity, He made all those things clear beforehand for us, so that we should not be wrecked on the reefs of adherence to their Law.

OF APPROACHING JUDGEMENT; A WARNING

4. What we must do, then, is to survey the present situation in all its aspects, and see which of them offers assurance of salvation for us. Let us keep ourselves with the utmost strictness from any kind of wrongdoing; otherwise wrongdoing will get the better of us. Let there be hatred in us for the errors of this world, so that there may be love for us in the world to come. We must not give such rein to our natural instincts that we feel ourselves free to mix at will with rogues and sinners, or we shall only grow to resemble them ourselves. The last great Hindrance of all [2] is now at hand, which according to Enoch is alluded to in the text, *the Lord has made an end of times and days, so that his Beloved can come quickly and enter upon his inheritance.*[*] The prophet Daniel, too, speaks to the same effect: *Ten kingdoms will reign over the earth, and after that a petty king will arise and bring down three of those kings at once.*[†] On the same subject Daniel has a similar thought: *I saw the fourth beast, which was evil and powerful and more savage than all the other creatures in the ocean; and I saw how ten horns sprang out of it; and then out of them sprang a smaller horn, a kind of offshoot, and it subdued three of the larger horns at once.*[‡] It is for you to think out the interpretation of this.[3]

There is another piece of advice that I would urge on you — speaking as one of your own kind, who loves each and every one of you more than his own life — and that is, that in the present circumstances you should take serious thought for yourselves, and not copy certain individuals by exaggerating your own sins and claiming that 'the Jews' Covenant is for us as well'. Indeed it is; for Moses had hardly received it when they forfeited it for ever. What Scripture tells us is, *Moses was in the mount forty*

* Not found in our Book of Enoch.   † *Daniel* vii, 24.
‡ *Daniel* vii, 7.

*days and forty nights fasting, and he received the covenant from
the Lord: tables of stone, written upon by the finger of the
Lord.** But because they then turned aside after idols, they lost
it. The Lord's words were, *Moses, Moses, make haste and get
down, for the people you brought out of Egypt have broken my
law.*† Moses understood, and threw down the two tables he
was holding; and that Covenant of theirs was smashed to pieces,
so that the seal of the Covenant of Jesus the Beloved might be
stamped on our own hearts, together with the hope that accom-
panies faith in Him.

(There is a great deal I should like to say here – not as a
teacher, but simply as one whose love for you feels it wrong to
leave out anything that is within our grasp – but this letter is
being written in haste, in my humble devotion to you.)

Accordingly, let us be specially wary in these final days, for
all our past years of faith will be no good to us if now, in these
lawless times and in face of the many trials that lie ahead of us,
we fail to offer such resistance as becomes God's children to the
insidious infiltration of the Dark One. We must set our faces
against any unprofitable trifling, and have a rooted aversion to
the Way of Wickedness and its works.

All the same, you are not to withdraw into yourselves and
live in solitude, as though God had already pronounced you
holy. Come and take your full share in the meetings, and in
deliberating for the common good. Scripture says, *Woe betide
those who are wise in their own eyes, and knowledgeable in
their own sight.*‡ Let us be men of the spirit, then; let us make
ourselves into a real temple of God. So far as lies in us, let us
devote ourselves to practising the fear of God and trying
earnestly to keep His commandments; and then His ordinances
will be our delight. For when the Lord judges the world there
is going to be no partiality; everyone will be recompensed in
proportion to what he has done. If he is a good man, his
righteousness will make the way smooth before him; but if he
is a bad man, the wages of his wickedness will be waiting to
confront him. So no assumption that we are among the called

* *Exodus* xxxiv, 28.   † ibid. xxxii, 7.   ‡ *Isaiah* v, 21.

197

must ever tempt us to relax our efforts, or fall asleep in our sins; otherwise the Prince of Evil will obtain control over us, and oust us from the kingdom of the Lord. Moreover, there is this to bear in mind, my brothers: when you see that even after such great signs and wonders had been wrought in Israel, they were none the less rejected, let us be very careful not to be found among those of whom it is written that *many are called, but few are chosen.**

OF THE INCARNATION AND PASSION OF CHRIST

5. Now, when the Lord resigned Himself to deliver His body to destruction, the aim He had in view was to sanctify us by the remission of our sins; which is effected by the sprinkling of His blood. For what Scripture says of Him (referring partly to Israel, but also partly to ourselves) is, *he was wounded on account of our transgressions, and bruised because of our sins, and by his scars we were healed. He was led to the slaughter like a sheep, and like a lamb that is dumb before its shearer.*† How deep should be our gratitude to the Lord, who thus gives us an insight into the past, as well as wisdom for the present and even a measure of understanding of the future! *Not without justice*, truly, as Scripture says, *are the nets spread for the birds*;‡ implying that ruin justly awaits a man if, when the Way of Holiness is known to him, he nevertheless turns his steps into the Way of Darkness.

The next point, my brothers, is this. Granted that the Lord was ready to undergo suffering in His concern for our life, yet He is, after all, the Lord of all the earth, to whom at the foundation of the world God had addressed the words, *Let us make man, in our own image and likeness.*§ In that case, how could He possibly bring Himself to suffer at the hands of men? Listen, and you shall hear. The prophets, graciously inspired by Himself, had been foretelling Him in their prophecies; and since it

* *Matthew* xx, 16.   † *Isaiah* liii, 5, 7.   ‡ *Proverbs* i, 17.   § *Genesis* i, 26.

was essential for Him – if He were indeed to destroy death and prove that the dead can rise again – to make an appearance in human flesh, He accordingly allowed Himself to suffer. By so doing, He would be able both to fulfil the promises that had been made to our ancestors, and to establish a new People for Himself; and also to make it clear, during His presence on earth, that it was His intention to raise mankind from the dead, and afterwards to judge them. Besides, by His teachings to the people of Israel and His working of miracles and wonders, He was making known His message and the infinite depths of His love. But it was in His choice of the Apostles, who were to preach His Gospel, that He truly showed Himself the Son of God; for those men were ruffians of the deepest dye,[4] which proved that He *came not to call saints, but sinners.**

Furthermore, supposing that He had not come in the flesh, how could it then have been possible for men ever to 'look on Him and be saved?' – for even when they behold the sun, though it is but His own handiwork and must one day cease to exist, they cannot look directly into its beams.

The Incarnation of the Son of God was intended to bring to a head the sins of the people who had persecuted and slain His prophets; and for this purpose He allowed Himself to suffer. For God lays the bruising of His flesh at their door, with the words, *When they buffet their own shepherd, the sheep of the flock shall perish.*† Even the actual form of His Passion He willingly embraced, since the word of prophecy had doomed Him to meet His death on a Tree. *Spare my life from the sword,*‡ it said; and then *Pierce my body with nails, for the congregation of the wicked have risen up against me;* § and again it says, *See, I have tendered my back to scourgings and my cheeks to blows, and I have set my face as firm as a rock.*‖

6. Moreover, after He had done as it was commanded Him, what does He say then? *Who presumes to accuse me? Let him stand up to face me. Who seeks a verdict against me? Let him approach the presence of the Lord's servant. Woe betide you!*

* *Mark* ii, 17.   † *Zechariah* xiii, 7.   ‡ *Psalm* xxii, 20.
§ ibid. 16.   ‖ *Isaiah* l, 6, 7.

*you shall all wear out like a garment, and the moth shall eat you away.** In another place the same prophet, viewing Him as some great strong block of marble laid ready for the trimming, says, *Look, I will lay a stone of great price in the foundations of Zion, a choice and precious cornerstone.* And how does he go on? *Whoever believes in it will have eternal life.*† Are we really to pin our hopes to a stone, then? Of course not; what is signified is the enduring strength with which the Lord has endued His human body; *he has set me,* He says, *like a solid block of stone.*‡ Elsewhere, too, the prophet says, *the stone which the builders rejected has become the cornerstone*; adding, *this is the great and wonderful day which the Lord has made,*§ (I am writing very simply, out of my humble devotion to you, so that you may understand [5]). And what does he say further? *A gathering of wicked men surrounded me; they came about me like bees round a honeycomb,*‖ and also, *they cast lots for my garments.*¶ It being His destiny to appear and to suffer in human flesh, this is the way his Passion was revealed beforehand; and the prophet says of the Jews, *Woe to their souls; they have planned a wicked scheme to their own hurt, saying, Let us bind the Just One in fetters, for he is a vexation to us.***

OF THE GOOD LAND OF MILK AND HONEY

Again, what has that other prophet, Moses, to say to them? *Look, this is what the Lord God says: Enter into the good land which the Lord vowed He would give to Abraham and Isaac and Jacob; take it for your inheritance, it is a land flowing with milk and honey.*†† Now let me show you what true insight can tell us about that. What it is, in fact, saying is, 'Put your hopes in that Joshua [6] who shall be shown to you in mortal guise'. For here the 'land' – that poor suffering creature – stands for 'man'; since it was out of earth that the shaping of Adam was wrought. What, then, is signified by a land that is 'good, and

---

* *Isaiah* l, 6, 7.
† *Isaiah* xxviii, 16.   ‡ ibid. l, 7.   § *Ps.* cxviii, 22.   ‖ ibid. 12.
¶ *Ps.*xxii, 18.   ** *Wisdom* ii, 12; *Isaiah* iii, 9.   †† *Exodus* xxxiii, 1, 3.

flowing with milk and honey?' (Blessings on the Lord, my brothers, for vouchsafing to us wisdom and the discernment of His secrets! The prophet is speaking in a Divine figure here, though only a sagacious and instructed lover of the Lord would understand it.) Well, when He turned us into new men by the remission of our sins, it made us into men of a wholly different stamp – having so completely the souls of little children that it seemed as though He had created us all over again. It is with reference to this re-fashioning that Scripture makes Him say to His Son, *Let us make man in our own image and likeness; and let them rule over the beasts of the earth and the fowls of the air and the fishes of the sea*; adding, as He contemplated the fair beauty of our fashioning, *Increase, and multiply, and fill the earth.** He was speaking then to His Son, but let me point out how He also speaks to ourselves. Having indeed brought about a second Creation in these last days, the Lord says, *Behold, I am now making the last things, even as I made the first.*† So this is what the prophet was referring to when he proclaimed, *Enter into a land flowing with milk and honey, and rule over it*; for you and I, you see, have actually been made completely new creatures. As He says in yet another of the prophets, *Behold, says the Lord, I will take the stony hearts out of this people* (the people, that is, who were already being foreseen by the Spirit) *and put hearts of flesh into them,*‡ which He says because He was going to appear in flesh Himself, and make His dwelling among us. Hence, my brothers, this poor habitation of our hearts is a shrine of holiness to the Lord! And moreover, the Lord says, *Where shall I appear before the Lord my God and be glorified?*§ and the reply is, *In the assembly of my brethren I will make confession to you; in the midst of the assembled people of God I will sing hymns to you.*‖ It is we ourselves, then, who are the people He has brought into the 'good land'.

And what does the 'milk and honey' signify? Well, a child's life begins first of all on milk, and then goes on afterwards to

* *Genesis* i, 26, 28.   † Not found in Scripture.   ‡ *Ezekiel* xi, 19.
§ *Ps.* xlii, 2.   ‖ *Ps.* xxii, 25.

honey; and in the same way we, after we have entered into life through belief in the promise and through the Word, shall then go on to live and become rulers of the earth [7] – as He said above, *let them increase and multiply, and rule over ... the fishes.* Is there anyone today, though, with this power to rule the beasts and fishes and fowls of the air? No; for we have to realize that ruling requires authority, if it is to issue commands and exercise dominion; and at present this is not the case. However, He has told us when it will be so: namely, when we have been made sufficiently perfect to become the inheritors of the Lord's Covenant.

7. Bear in mind, then, O children of joy, that there is not a single thing which the Lord in His goodness has not made clear to us beforehand, so that we may know to whom all our thanks and praises are due. Though the Son of God was the divine Lord, and the future Judge of living and dead alike, yet nevertheless He suffered, in order that His affliction might win life for us. So we have to accept the fact that, if it had not been on our behalf, it would have been impossible for the Son of God to experience suffering.

OF THE VINEGAR AND THE GALL

You may ask next why He was given vinegar and gall to drink at His crucifixion. Hear, then, how there had already been a prefiguring of this, in the case of the Temple priesthood. The Scriptural precept was, *Whoever fails to keep the Fast [8] shall die the death;* * which was a commandment given by the Lord in reference to the fact that in time to come He would be sacrificing the vessel of His Spirit for our sins – whereby the type created in Isaac, when he was sacrificed on the altar, would find its fulfilment. And what does it say in the prophet? *Let them eat of the goat [9] which is offered for their sins at the fast, and* (note this carefully) *let all the priests, but nobody else, eat of its inward parts, unwashed and with vinegar.†* Why was this? Because 'when I am about to offer My Body for the sins of this

* *Leviticus* xxiii, 29.
† Not in Scripture; perhaps an extract from the Jewish regulations.

new People of Mine, you will be giving Me gall and vinegar to drink. That is why you shall be the only ones to eat, while the people of Israel are fasting and lamenting in sackcloth and ashes'. In this way He indicated His predestined sufferings at their hands.

OF THE SCAPEGOAT

Notice the directions He gave. *Take a couple of goats, unblemished and well-matched; bring them for an offering, and let the priest take one of them for a burnt-offering.** And what are they to do with the other? *The other*, He declares, *is accursed*. (Now see how plainly the type of Jesus appears.) *Spit on it, all of you; thrust your goads into it, wreathe its head with scarlet wool, and so let it be driven out into the desert.* This is done, and the goat-ward leads the animal into the desert, where he takes off the wool and leaves it there, on the bush we call a bramble (the plant we usually eat the berries of, if we come across it in the countryside; nothing has such tasty fruit as a bramble). Now what does that signify? Notice that the first goat is for the altar, and the other is accursed; and that it is the accursed one that wears the wreath. That is because they shall see Him on That Day clad to the ankles in His red woollen robe, and will say, 'Is not this he whom we once crucified, and mocked and pierced and spat upon? Yes, this is the man who told us that he was the son of God.' But how will He resemble the goat? The point of there being two similar goats, both of them fair and alike, is that when they see Him coming on the Day, they are going to be struck with terror at the manifest parallel between Him and the goat. In this ordinance, then, you are to see typified the future sufferings of Jesus.

But why should they put the wool on the thorns? This too is a type of Jesus, meant for the Church's instruction. For if one wanted to take the scarlet wool for himself, it would cost him much suffering, since the thorns were fearsome and could only

* *Leviticus* xvi, 5ff.

203

be mastered with anguish. Similarly, says He, those who would behold Me and possess My kingdom must go through affliction and suffering before they can reach Me.

OF THE WATER OF PURIFICATION

8. What now, do you suppose, is the significance of His next direction to the Jews? Men whose sins had come to a head were to bring a heifer for an offering, and slay it and burn it. Then, after gathering up the ashes and putting them into basins of water, young children were to tie scarlet wool on branches of wood (here again, you see, we have the scarlet wool and the type of the Cross), together with sprigs of hyssop; and with these the people were to be sprinkled, man by man, by the youngsters, to cleanse them from their sins. See how clearly He is speaking to you here! The calf is Jesus, and the sinners who offer it are those who dragged Him to the slaughter. After that we hear no more of the men, or of glory in store for sinners. The children with the sprinklers are our own Gospel preachers of sin forgiven and hearts made clean, to whom He gave authority to proclaim the Good News, and of whom, as a token of the tribes, there were a dozen, because the tribes of Israel were twelve. And why were there a trio of boys to do the sprinkling? That was in memory of Abraham, Isaac and Jacob, and their greatness in the sight of God. And why was the wool put on living wood? Because the royal realm of Jesus is founded on a Tree, and they who hope in Him shall have eternal life. And why hyssop as well as wool? Because in His reign there will be days that are evil and corrupt, through which we shall come to our salvation; and also because slime of hyssop is a remedy for bodily aches and pains. To ourselves it is plain enough that these were the true reasons for doing things in this way; but to them it was all dark, because their ears were deaf to the voice of the Lord.

OF CIRCUMCISION

9. He has something to say, in fact, in another place about those ears, when He speaks of His circumcising of our hearts. In the prophet the Lord says, *As soon as their ears heard of me, they obeyed me;* * and again, *they that are afar off shall hear with their ears, and know what I have done;* † and, *Be circumcised in your hearts says the Lord.*‡ Again, He says, *Hear, O Israel; these are the words of the Lord your God.*§ And again, the Spirit of the Lord proclaims, *Who is he that desires to live for ever? Let his ears be open to the voice of my servant.*‖ Once more, He says, *Hear, O heavens, and give ear, O earth, for the Lord has spoken this for a testimony.*¶ He says also, *Hear the word of the Lord, you princes of this people.*** And yet again, He says, *Hear, my children, the voice of one crying in the wilderness.*†† In short, He circumcised our ears,[10] so that we might hear His word and believe.

The particular form of circumcision in which they put their trust, however, has been completely set aside, for He has declared that circumcision is not a physical thing. That is where they went wrong, because they had been misled by an evil angel. God's actual words to them were, *Thus says the Lord your God* – and this is where I find His commandment – *do not plant your seed among thorns, but be circumcised for the Lord.*‡‡ What is His meaning? Why, *circumcise the hardness of your hearts, and do not be so stiffnecked.*§§ Or again, take this : *See, says the Lord, all those nations are uncircumcised in their foreskins, but this people is uncircumcised in its heart.*‖‖ You will say, 'But surely this people received physical circumcision as the seal of their Covenant?' Why, every Syrian and every Arab is physically circumcised, and so are the idol-priesthoods; but does that make them members of the Jews' Covenant? Even the very Egyptians practise physical circumcision.

Dear children of love, here is the full explanation of it all.

* *Ps.* xviii, 44. † *Isaiah* xxxiii, 13. ‡ *Jeremiah* iv, 4. § ibid. vii, 2.
‖ *Ps.* xxxiv, 11, 12. ¶ *Isaiah* i, 2. ** ibid. i, 10. †† ibid. xl, 3.
‡‡ *Jeremiah* iv, 3. §§ *Deuteronomy* x, 16. ‖‖ *Jeremiah* ix, 26.

Circumcision was given to us in the first place by Abraham; but he, when he circumcised himself, did so in a spiritual prevision of Jesus. He got his instruction from three letters of the alphabet; [11] for the Scripture tells us that *out of his own household Abraham circumcised eighteen and three hundred.** How does his spiritual intuition come into this? Well, notice how it specifies the eighteen first; and then, separately from this, the three hundred. Now, in writing eighteen, the ten is expressed by the letter I and the eight by E; and there, you see, you have I E (sus). And then, since grace was to come by a Cross, of which T is the shape, it adds 'and three hundred'. Thus it indicates 'Jesus' with two of the letters, and 'the Cross' with the third. All this is perfectly well known to Him who has graciously planted the seeds of His teaching in our hearts; and a better interpretation than this I have never given to anybody. I am persuaded, though, that you have every right to know it.

OF THE LAWS OF DIET

10. And now for that saying of Moses, *You are not to eat of swine; nor yet of eagle, hawk, or crow; nor of any fish that has not got scales.*† In this there are three distinct moral precepts which he had received and understood. (For God says in Deuteronomy, *I will make a covenant with this people that will embody my rules for holiness;*‡ so, you see, the Divine command is in no sense a literal ban on eating, and Moses was speaking spiritually.) The meaning of his allusion to swine is this: what he is really saying is, 'you are not to consort with the class of people who are like swine, inasmuch as they forget all about the Lord while they are living in affluence, but remember Him when they are in want – just as a swine, so long as it is eating, ignores its master, but starts to squeal the moment it feels hungry, and then falls silent again when it is given food.'

Next, *you shall eat neither eagle nor hawk, kite nor crow.*

---

* *Genesis* xiv, 14; xvii, 23.
† *Leviticus* xi; *Deuteronomy* xiv.   ‡ *Deuteronomy* iv, 1.

This means that you are not to frequent the company nor imitate the habits of those who have no idea of earning their own bread by toil and sweat, but in total disregard of all law swoop down on the possessions of other people; going about with every appearance of innocence, but keeping a sharp lookout and darting glances in every direction to see whom their rapacity can prey upon next. In the same way, the birds he speaks of are the only ones that do not provide their own food; sitting indolently on their perches, they watch for an opportunity to devour the flesh of other creatures, and make themselves thorough-going pests by their graceless ways.

When he says, *you are not to eat of the lamprey, the polypus, or the cuttlefish,* his meaning is that you are not to consort with or imitate the kind of people who have rejected God altogether, and are already living under sentence of death; just as it is those fish, and no others, which are doomed to swim far down in the lowest depths of ocean, never breaking surface like the rest, but making their homes underground at the bottom of the sea.

(Among other things, he also says, *you are not to eat of the hare,** by which he means you are not to debauch young boys, or become like those who do; because the hare grows a fresh orifice in its backside every year, and has as many of these holes as the years of its life. And *you are not to eat the hyena*† signifies that you are to be no lecher or libertine, or copy their ways; for that creature changes its sex annually and is a male at one time and a female at another. The weasel, too, he speaks of with abhorrence, and not without good reason; his implication being that you are not to imitate those who, we are told, are filthy enough to use their mouths for the practice of vice, nor to frequent the abandoned women who do the same – since it is through its mouth that this animal is impregnated.)

In these dietary laws, then, Moses was taking three moral maxims and expounding them spiritually; though the Jews, with their carnal instincts, took him to be referring literally to foodstuffs. David, too, had been given understanding of the

* *Leviticus* xi, 6.   † Not in the O.T.

same three principles; but how he expresses them is, *Blessed is the man who has not followed the counsel of the godless* (like the fishes that take their way in darkness down to the depths below), *nor taken his stand in the path of sinners* (like those who indulge their swinish sins behind a God-fearing appearance), *and has not sat in the seat of the predators** (like the birds that sit waiting for their prey). So now you have the whole truth about these alimentary precepts.

Moses did say, however, that *you may eat anything that has cloven hoofs and chews the cud.** Why does he say this? Because when a creature of that kind is given provender, it shows its recognition of the giver, and takes an evident pleasure in him while it is refreshing itself. So Moses, contemplating what the Lord required, gave it this apt turn of expression. For what those words of his mean is, 'seek the company of men who fear the Lord; who muse in their hearts on the purport of every word they have received; who take the statutes of the Lord on their lips, and observe them; who know that meditation is a delight – who do, in fact, *chew the cud* of the Lord's word'. And the *cloven hoof*? That means that a good man is at one and the same time walking in this present world and also anticipating the holiness of eternity. So you see what a master of lawgiving Moses was. His own people did not see or understand these things – how could they? – but we understand his directions rightly, and interpret them as the Lord intended. Indeed, it was to aid our comprehension of them that He 'circumcised' our ears and our hearts.

OF BAPTISM AND OF THE CROSS [12]

11. Now let us see if the Lord has been at any pains to give us a foreshadowing of the waters of baptism, and of the Cross. Regarding the former, we have the evidence of Scripture that Israel would refuse to accept the washing which confers remission of sins, and would set up a substitute of their own instead.[13] *Be astonished, you heavens,* says the prophet, *and*

* *Ps.* i, l.   † *Leviticus* xi, 3; *Deuteronomy* xiv, 6.

let the earth shudder more and more, at the two wicked things this people has done; they have turned their backs on me, the fountain of life, and they have dug a well of doom for themselves. Is Sinai, my holy mountain, a rock that has been deserted, then? As a bird's fledglings shall you be, which go fluttering hither and thither when they are bereft of their proper nest.* And again the prophet says, *I will go on before you, levelling mountains, shattering gates of brass and sundering bolts of iron, and I will give you treasures that are mysterious,*[14] *secret, and unseen, so that you may know me for the Lord God.*† Also, *You shall dwell on high in a rocky fastness, where there are springs of never-failing water; your eyes shall see the King in glory, and your heart shall ponder the fear of the Lord.*‡ And in another prophet He says, *He that does these things shall be like a tree planted where the streams divide, with fruit springing forth in its season and leaves that never fade, and all his doings shall prosper. Not so with the godless; no, they shall be like dust that is swept from the face of the earth by the gales. Therefore the godless shall not be able to stand at the Judgment, nor sinners in the council of the righteous; for the Lord knows the way of the righteous, but the way of the godless shall be utterly destroyed.*§ Observe there how He describes both the water and the Cross in the same figure; His meaning is, 'Blessed are those who go down into the water with their hopes set on the Cross'. In speaking of their reward *in its season*, He means to say 'I will pay it in time to come'; but in the meanwhile, leaves *that never fade* means that every word your lips utter in faith and love will open the gate of conversion and hope to many.

Another of the prophets also says, *the land of Jacob was extolled above all the earth;*|| which signifies that He raises to glory the earthen vessel that contains His Spirit.[15] What more does He say? *There was a river issuing from the right hand, with fair young trees rising out of it; and whoever eats of them shall have life for evermore.*¶ Here He is saying that after we

---

* *Isaiah* xvi, 1; *Jeremiah* ii, 13.   † ibid. xlv, 2.   ‡ ibid. xxxiii, 16-18.
§ *Ps.* i, 3-6. || *Ezekiel* xx, 6 (?).   ¶ ibid. xlvii, 1ff.

have stepped down into the water burdened with sin and de-filement, we come up out of it in full fruitage, with reverence in our hearts and the hope of Jesus in our souls; and *whoever eats of them shall have life for evermore* means that he who hears these sayings, and believes, will live for ever.

12. He also gives us an outline of the Cross in another of the prophets, who says, *When shall the consummation of all this be accomplished? says the Lord. When a tree droops and then rises up again; and when blood drips from a tree.** Here you have an allusion both to the Cross and to its future Victim. And in another place, when the Israelites were being assailed by the neighbouring tribesmen, there is the command He gave to Moses, for the purpose of reminding those under attack that their own sins were responsible for the loss of their lives. That was when the Spirit, speaking inwardly to Moses, prompted him to make a representation of the Cross and Him who was to suffer on it; which was His way of intimating that unless they come to put their hopes in Him, the hostilities against them will never cease. So Moses made a pile of shields, one upon another, in the midst of the fray; and taking his stand there, high above all the rest, he spread his two arms out wide, and Israel thereupon began to regain the victory. But every time he let them drop, death became their master again. Why was this? To make them see that their salvation must depend upon put-ting their trust in Him. Thus He says in another of the prophets, *All day long I stretched out my hands to a faithless people, and one that rejects my righteous way.*†

There was also another occasion on which Moses made a symbol of Jesus. It was to show how Jesus is ordained to suffer and to give life to men, in spite of their belief that they have destroyed Him. This sign took place at a time when there was heavy mortality among the Israelites; for in order to convince them that the result of their sinning must be to bring them into the bitterness of death, the Lord had caused them to be fatally bitten by all manner of serpents – it having been through a serpent that sin first came into the world, in the person of Eve.

* *II Esdras* iv, 33; v, 5.   † *Isaiah* lxv, 2.

So, even though Moses had personally given them the command, *you shall have no image, whether cast or carved, for your god,** yet now, to show them a symbol of Jesus, he constructed one himself. Moses made a serpent out of brass, set it up in a conspicuous position, and issued a proclamation summoning the people. When they came flocking together, entreating Moses to intercede for their healing, he told them, 'Whenever one of you is bitten, let him approach the serpent on the pole in a spirit of hope, believing that even though it is without life itself it has nevertheless power to impart life; and he will recover at once.' And that is what they did.† Here again you see the glory of Jesus; for there is nothing which is not found in Him, and nothing which does not point to Him.

And a further point; what is it that Moses says to Jesus-ben-Nave? [16] – that prophetic figure whom he so names for the sole purpose of letting the whole people learn how the Father reveals to us every detail that bears upon His Son. When Moses sent this Jesus-ben-Nave to spy out the land, he said (addressing him by that name), *Take a scroll in your hand and note down this word from the Lord: that in the last days the Son of God will destroy the whole house of Amalek root and branch.*‡ There again, you see, is Jesus; not as the son of a man, but as the Son of God – though here appearing, in a type, in human form. And because in after times they will assert that Christ is a son of David, David himself is inspired to say, in fear and understanding of this error of sinful men, *The LORD said to my lord, Sit here on my right hand, until I make your enemies a cushion to put your feet on.*§ (There is likewise the saying of Isaiah, *the LORD said to my anointed lord, I have taken hold of his right hand, for nations to bow in submission before him; and I will break down the might of kings.*||) Notice how David calls Him Lord; he does not call Him son.

* *Deuteronomy* xxvii, 15.   † *Numbers* xxi, 9.   ‡ *Exodus* xvii, 14.
§ *Ps.* cx, 1. || *Isaiah* xlv, 1.

OF THE PEOPLE OF THE COVENANT

13. Let us see now whether it is our own people or the earlier folk who are the true inheritors, and whether the Covenant is meant for us or for them. Listen to what Scripture has to say about 'the People'. *Isaac entreated the Lord for his wife Rebecca, because she was barren; and she conceived. Then Rebecca went to inquire of the Lord, and the Lord said to her, Two nations are in your womb, and two peoples in your bowels; one people shall be stronger than the other people, and the elder shall be servant to the younger.** Now then; it is for you to realize who Isaac is, and who Rebecca is, and to which people this prophecy of the superiority of one to the other refers.

The language of Jacob, in another prophecy, is even plainer, when he says to his son Joseph, *Behold, the Lord has not bereaved me of your presence; fetch me your sons, that I may give them my blessing.* Joseph fetched Ephraim and Manasseh; and since he wanted the blessing for Manasseh, as the elder of the two, he led him to the right hand of his father Jacob. But Jacob, with the eye of the spirit, could perceive the People of the future; and so what does it say? *Jacob changed his hands across, and laying his right hand on the head of Ephraim, the second and younger son, he gave the blessing to him. Joseph said to Jacob, Not so; put your right hand on Manasseh's head; it is he that is my first-born. But Jacob told Joseph, I know, child, I know; but the elder must serve the younger – though this one shall have a blessing too.*† So you can see who is meant by His decree that 'this People shall have the primacy, and inherit the Covenant'. And if, in addition to all this, we find further confirmation of it in the life of Abraham, it puts the final touch to our knowledge. For what was it that He said to Abraham, when he was accounted righteous for being the only believer? *See, Abraham, I have appointed you to be the ancestor of Gentile nations who believe in God but without being circumcised.*‡

14. Very well, then. Now let us see whether the Covenant, which He vowed to the patriarchs to give the People, was in fact

* *Genesis* xxv, 21, 23.   † ibid. xlviii, 9 ff.   ‡ ibid. xvii, 4.

so given. It was, to be sure; but their sins disqualified them for the possession of it. *Moses, the prophet tells us, spent forty days and forty nights fasting on mount Sinai, to get the Lord's covenant for the people. And Moses received the two tablets from the Lord, written in the Spirit by the finger of the Lord's hand.** Moses took these, and was carrying them down to give to the people, when the Lord said to Moses, *Moses, Moses, make haste and get down, for the people you brought out of Egypt have been breaking my law. And Moses perceived that they were making molten images for themselves again; and he threw away the tablets out of his hand, and the tablets of the Lord's covenant were broken to pieces.†* So although it was indeed given to Moses, they themselves lost their right to it.

Mark now how it came to belong to us. Moses was given it as a servant; but it was the Lord Himself who conferred it on us, making us the People of the Inheritance by His sufferings on our behalf. Though the purpose of the Incarnation was partly to allow them to put the final seal on their sins, it was also that we might receive the Covenant of the Lord Jesus from its rightful Heir. It was this for which He had been ordained: by manifesting Himself in person, to redeem from the murk of darkness our hearts (so long wasted by death and abandoned to the mischief of error) and to establish a covenant among us by His word. For Scripture tells us how the Father had charged Him to ransom us from the darkness, and create a holy People for Himself. *I, the Lord your God, have called you in righteousness,* the prophet says; *I will hold your hand and strengthen you, and I have appointed you to make a covenant with the people, and to be a light to the nations; to open the eyes of the blind, to loose the captives from their chains, and to free those that sit in darkness from their prison-house.‡* That is how we know the plight from which we have been redeemed. The prophet also says, *The Spirit of the Lord is upon me, because he has anointed me to preach glad tidings of grace to the lowly; he has sent me to heal the broken-hearted, to proclaim deliverance to prisoners and*

* *Exodus* xxiv, 18; xxxi, 18.   † ibid. xxxii, 7–19.
‡ *Isaiah* xlii, 6, 7.

*recovery of sight to the blind, to announce a year of divine
favour and a day of recompense, and to comfort all that mourn.**

OF THE SABBATH

15. Next, about the sabbath. In the Decalogue, when God spoke
to Moses face to face on mount Sinai, we read, *Also keep
the Lord's sabbath holy, with clean hands and a pure heart;*†
and in another place it says, *If my sons keep the sabbath, I will
show a mercy upon them.*‡ Now what is said at the very beginning of Creation about the sabbath, is this: *In six days God
created the works of his hands, and finished them on the seventh
day; and he rested on that day, and sanctified it*§ Notice particularly, my children, the significance of *he finished them in six
days.* What that means is, that He is going to bring the world to
an end in six thousand years, since with Him one day means a
thousand years; witness His own saying, *Behold, a day of the
Lord shall be as a thousand years.*‖ Therefore, my children, in
six days – six thousand years, that is – there is going to be an
end of everything. After that, *he rested on the seventh day* indicates that when His Son returns, He will put an end to the
Years of the Lawless One, pass sentence on the godless, trans-
form the sun and moon and stars, and then, on the seventh
Day, enter into His true rest.

You shall keep it holy, says He, *with clean hands and a pure
heart*. We are very much mistaken if there is anybody at the
present time with a heart pure enough to keep holy the day
which God has sanctified. Observe, though, that a time is coming
when we shall indeed rest and keep it holy – though not until
our final justification has enabled us to do so; that is, when the
promise has at last become ours, when iniquity is no more, and
when the Lord has made all things new. Then we shall be able
to keep it holy, because we ourselves will have been made holy
first.

He also tells them, *I have no patience with your new moons and*

* *Isaiah* lxi, 1, 2.   † *Exodus* xx, 8.   ‡ *Jeremiah* xvii, 24.
§ *Genesis* ii, 2.   ‖ *Ps.* xc, 4.

sabbaths.* You can see what He is saying there: 'It is not these sabbaths of the present age that I find acceptable, but the one of my own appointment: the one that, after I have set all things at rest, is to usher in the Eighth Day,[17] the commencement of a new world.' (And we too rejoice in celebrating the eighth day; because that was when Jesus rose from the dead, and showed Himself again, and ascended into heaven.)[18]

OF THE TEMPLE

16. We come now to the matter of the Temple; and I will show you how mistaken these miserable folk were in pinning their hopes to the building itself, as if that were the home of God, instead of to God their own Creator. Indeed, they were scarcely less misguided than the heathen in the way they ascribed Divine holiness to their Temple. For mark how completely the words of the Lord Himself dispense with it. *Who is it, who can span the whole heaven with the breadth of one hand, or the earth with the flat of his palm? Is it not I? says the Lord. The heaven is a throne for me, and the earth a stool for my feet. What sort of house, then, will you build for me, and where is the spot that can serve me for a resting-place?†* You can see that their hope was the purest folly. Besides, He also says, *Behold, those who pulled the Temple down shall rebuild it‡* – the very thing which is actually in process of fulfilment now; for after their armed rebellion it was demolished by their enemies, and now they themselves are about to build it up again, as subjects of their foemen. All the same, it has been revealed that city, Temple, and Jewish people are all alike doomed to perish one day; for Scripture says, *it will come to pass in the last days that the Lord will deliver up to destruction the sheep of the pasture, with their sheepfold and their watchtower.§* And for the Lord to say a thing is for that thing to come about.

But what we have to ask next is, Can there be any such thing

* *Isaiah* i, 13.   † ibid. lxvi, 1.
‡ ibid. xlix, 17 (LXX).   § *Enoch* lxxxix, 56.

as a temple of God at all? To be sure there can – but where He Himself tells us that He is building it and perfecting it. For it is written, *when the Week draws to its close, then a temple of God will be built gloriously in the Name of the Lord;*[*] and from this I must infer that there is indeed such a thing as a temple. Only, mark that it is to be *built in the Name of the Lord*; for in the days before we believed in God, our hearts were a rotten, shaky abode, and a temple only too truly built with hands, since by our persistent opposition to God we had made them into a chamber of idolatry and a home for demons. Now *it will be built in the Name of the Lord*. Make sure, too, that this temple of the Lord shall be built *gloriously*, and listen to the way in which this can be done. When we were granted remission of our sins, and came to put our hopes in His Name, we were made new men, created all over again from the beginning; and as a consequence of that, God is at this moment actually dwelling within us in that poor habitation of ours. How so? Why, in the message of His Faith, and in the call of His promise; in the wisdom of His statutes, and the precepts of His teaching; in His own very Presence inwardly inspiring us, and dwelling within us; in His unlocking of the temple doors of our lips, and His gift to us of repentance. It is by these ways that He admits us, the bondsmen of mortality, into the Temple that is immortal. For when a man is earnestly bent on salvation, his eyes are not on his fellow-man,[19] but on the One who is dwelling in that person and speaking through him; and he is full of wonder that never till now has he heard such words from Him, nor known the desire of hearing them. This is what the building up of a spiritual temple to the Lord means.

17. I hope with all my heart that, so far as a simple and straightforward exposition is possible, I have at least omitted nothing that bears directly upon our salvation. For if my pen were once to start on the theme of the present era, or of those that are to come, you would never understand; for such things are veiled in the language of parable. So let this be enough.

[*] Source unknown; possibly an allusion to *Daniel* ix, 24?

THE TWO WAYS[20]

18. Now let us pass on to quite a different sort of instruction and knowledge. There are two Ways of teaching, and two wielders of power; one of light and the other of darkness. Between those two Ways there is a vast difference, because over the one are posted the light-bearing angels of God, and over the other the angels of Satan; and one of these two is the Lord from all eternity to all eternity, while the other stands paramount over this present age of iniquity.

THE WAY OF LIGHT

19. First, then, for the Way of Light; and here a man who would make the pilgrimage to his appointed home must put his whole heart into his work. To aid our steps on the road, illumination has been given to us then – Love your Maker; fear your Creator; give glory to Him who redeemed you from death. Practise singleness of heart, and a richness of the spirit. Shun the company of those who walk in the Way of Death. Abhor anything that is displeasing to God, and hold every form of hypocrisy in detestation. Be sure that you never depart from the commandments of the Lord.

Do not exaggerate your own importance, but be modest at all points, and never claim credit for yourself. Cherish no ill-natured designs upon your neighbour. Forbid yourself any appearance of presumption. Commit no fornication, adultery, or unnatural vice. Never take the word of God on your lips in loose company. If you have to rebuke anyone for a fault, do it without fear or favour. Keep calm and mild; reverence the words you have heard, and bear no resentment towards a brother.

Never be in two minds as to whether something is or is not to be. Never make free with the Name of the Lord. Never do away with an unborn child, or destroy it after its birth. Do not withhold your hand from your son or your daughter, but bring them up in the fear of God from their childhood.

Do not cast covetous eyes on a neighbour's possessions. Do not be greedy for gain. Do not set your heart on being intimate with the great, but look for the company of people who are humble and virtuous. Whatever experience comes your way, accept it as a blessing, in the certainty that nothing can happen without God.

Never equivocate, either in thought or speech. Obey your masters with respectfulness and fear, as the representatives of God. Do not speak sharply when you are giving orders to servants, whether men or women, if their trust is in the same God as yours; else they may lose their fear of Him who is over you both. The Lord did not come to call people according to their rank; He came for those who were already prepared by the Spirit.

Give your neighbour a share of all you have, and do not call anything your own. If you and he participate together in things immortal, how much more so in things that are mortal? Never be in a hurry to speak, for the tongue is a fatal snare. For your soul's sake, be as pure as you can.

Do not be one of those who stretch out their hands to take, but draw back when the time comes for giving. Cherish as the apple of your eye anyone who expounds the word of the Lord to you.

Day and night keep the Day of Judgement in mind. Seek the company of God's people every day; either labouring by word of mouth – that is to say, by going among them for purposes of exhortation, and striving to save souls by the power of speech – or else working with your hands, to earn a ransom for your own sins.

Never hesitate to give; and when you are giving, do it without grumbling; you will soon find out Who can be generous with His rewards. Keep the traditions you have received, without making any additions or deductions of your own. Never cease to detest evil. Make your decisions fairly and uprightly.

Do nothing to encourage dissensions. Bring the disputants together, and compose their quarrel. And make confession of your own faults; you are not to come to prayer with a bad conscience.

That is the Way of Light.

THE WAY OF DARKNESS

20. The Way of the Dark Lord is devious and fraught with damnation. It is the way to death and eternal punishment. In it is found all that destroys the souls of men: idol-worship, brazen self-assertion, and the arrogance of power; cant and duplicity; adultery, manslaughter, and robbery; vanity, rascality, sharp practice, spitefulness and contumacy; sorcery and black magic; greed, and defiance of God. They persecute the virtuous; they hate truth and love falsehood; they know nothing of the rewards of righteousness, or of devotion to goodness and just judgement. The widow and the orphan are nothing to them; and their sleepless nights are spent, not in fearing God, but in the pursuit of vice. Gentleness and patience are altogether alien to them; all they care for is paltry and worthless, all they look for is their own advantage. They have no pity for the poor, nor ever trouble their heads about any poor soul in distress. They are always ready with malicious rumours, for knowledge of their Creator is not in them. They make away with infants, destroying the image of God; they turn the needy from their doors, and deal harshly with the afflicted; while they aid and abet the rich, they are brutal in their judgement of the poor. In a word, they are utterly and altogether sunk in sin.

CONCLUSION

21. All this shows what a good thing it is to have learnt the precepts of the Lord, as they are set forth in Scripture, and to put them into practice. For the man who does this, there will be glory in the kingdom of God; but one who prefers the other Way will perish together with his works. (To this end are the ordinances of resurrection and retribution.)

And here, if you will accept a hint from a well-wisher, I have an appeal to make to those of you who are in positions of influence. You have some amongst you to whom you could do good – pray see that you do not fail them.

The day is approaching when the world will share the fate of the Evil One. *The Lord is at hand, and his reward with him.** So once again I must urge you; be yourselves your own good lawgivers, be yourselves your own trusty counsellors, and have no more to do with the piety of hypocrites. May the God and Lord of all the world grant you wisdom, understanding, and knowledge, together with true comprehension of His ordinances, and the gift of perseverance. Take God for your teacher, and study to learn what the Lord requires of you; then do it, and you will find yourselves accepted at the Day of Judgement.

If good deeds are ever remembered, have a thought for me and think these things over. Then my anxiety and my hours of wakefulness may at least have produced something that is good. I ask this as an act of grace from you. So long as the fair vessel of the flesh remains to you, try to leave none of these things undone; spend continual study on them, and see that all the commandments are carried out faithfully. They are assuredly worth the pains; which is why I was the more solicitous to put my best efforts into this letter, in the hope that it might do something to improve your spirits.

Farewell, my children of love and peace. May the Lord of glory and of all grace be with your spirit.

NOTES

1. As suggested in the Preface, probably the contemporary resurgence of Judaism.

2. Apparently a reference to the Antichrist whose coming heralded the end of the world.

3. It is clear that these visions of Daniel are understood by Barnabas to be prophetic descriptions of certain emperors of Rome, the little horn being evidently the Antichrist. Though prudence prevents

* *Isaiah* xl, 10.

him from explicitly identifying them, he feels that his readers will have no difficulty in doing so. Today, however, the commentators are at variance in their efforts to find a satisfactory interpretation.

4. A shocking exaggeration? No doubt; though not altogether groundless. (The records of Judas, Matthew, and Paul come to mind.) Christ's partiality for publicans and sinners was notorious.

5. Lucidity is not one of Barnabas' gifts, but his argument seems to be: We men have been re-made by the Lord into a new and better form, as Christians (for God's words to His Son, 'Let us make man in Our own image, etc', were about ourselves, not about mankind in general); and since 'earth' allegorically signifies 'man', so this re-creation into a better state is described as 'entering into a good land flowing with milk and honey'.

6. Joshua, who led the Israelites into the Promised Land, is a well-known type of Jesus. In Hebrew the two names are the same.

7. In the final regeneration (*Matthew* xix, 28) the lordship of creation, forfeited by Adam after the Fall, will be resumed by God's elect.

8. The Levitical fast is regarded as a type of Christ's afflictions. By 'the vessel of His Spirit' is meant His body.

9. Reference to *Leviticus* xvi and xxiii, where the ceremonies of the Day of Atonement are prescribed, will show that many of the details mentioned here by Barnabas are unknown to Scripture. Nothing is said there, for example, of the similarity of the two goats, or of the spitting and goading, or of the scarlet wool, or of the bramble bush; and whereas Barnabas declares that the second goat is eaten by the priests, the Levitical directions are for the whole carcase to be burnt outside the camp. The discrepancies may be due to the difference between the biblical description of the rite and its actual performance according to later Jewish tradition.

10. The idea of a spiritual circumcision of the ear is found in *Jeremiah* vi, 10; but why Barnabas extends it to the various texts he quotes here is not clear.

11. i.e. The letters IET, which in Greek stand for the numerals 318. Barnabas has been over hasty, though, in his zeal for allegorizing; for 318 was not, as he alleges, the number of men who were circumcised by Abraham – the supposed quotation to this effect existing only in Barnabas' imagination – but the number of slaves born in his household (*Genesis* xiv, 14). Those whom he actually circumcised must have been more numerous than these, since they also included some whom

he had purchased elsewhere (ibid. xvii, 23). In any case, if Barnabas had not been so accustomed to using a Greek translation of the Bible, he would have remembered that in the original Hebrew text numbers are of course not represented by Greek letters at all.

12. It will help the reader's understanding of this section to bear in mind that in allegorizing the scriptures any mention of water may be taken to prefigure baptism, and any mention of wood or trees to prefigure the Cross.

13. He means the ceremonious ablutions prescribed by Jewish tradition (cf. *Mark* vii, 3-5).

14. i.e. the spiritual graces conferred by baptism.

15. Barnabas explains this as a prophecy of the Resurrection. The 'earthen vessel containing His Spirit' is His body (cf. the similar expressions in chs. vii and xxi).

16. *Jesus-ben-Nave* is the Joshua-son-of-Nun of English Bibles.

17. According to Barnabas, five 'days' (i.e. 5000 years) had already passed, and he and his contemporaries were living in the sixth 'day'. After this would come the seventh 'day', or Millennium, when Christ would descend in glory and reign for 1000 years on earth. Then would follow the end of the world (the 'setting of all things at rest') and the dawning of the Eighth Day, the day of eternity. Meantime, in the more mundane sphere, the conclusion of every seven-day week is followed by an 'eighth' day which is the first of the succeeding week, and is known to us as Sunday, the day commemorating the Resurrection.

18. Barnabas probably believed the Resurrection and the Ascension to have occurred on the same day.

19. i.e. his Christian instructor.

20. The remainder of the Epistle, with the exception of the concluding chapter, is taken from the 'Two Ways' of the *Didache*.

*

THE DIDACHE

*

The Didache

In 1873 a small volume of 120 parchment leaves, written in Greek in the year 1056, was found in the library of a Constantinople monastery. In it, in addition to the Epistles of Barnabas and Clement and a collection of the letters of Ignatius, there was a composition which, on its publication to the world ten years later, was quickly recognized as the most important discovery of modern times for students of Christian antiquity. It was entitled *The Teaching of the Lord to the Gentiles, through the Twelve Apostles*, though for convenience it is known nowadays simply as *The Didache* (i.e. the Teaching). The contents of it fall into two separate and distinct divisions; the first, known as The Two Ways, consists of an exposition of Christian morality, setting forth the various virtues and vices which respectively compose the Way of Life and the Way of Death, while the second is a compendium of rules dealing with such aspects of Church life as baptism, fasting, the Eucharist, itinerant missionaries, local ministers, and so forth.

It had long been known that such a work existed, for there are references to it in several ancient writers. Eusebius, for example, makes mention of it;* Clement of Alexandria cites it as 'scripture';† Athanasius recommends it for the use of catechists,‡ and a passage from it has been identified in the prayerbook of his contemporary Serapion. From the circumstance that the three last-named are all natives of Alexandria, and from certain indications in the text, it has been inferred that the *Didache* itself may have originated in that city.

Nothing is known of the author. The date of the work has been a matter of dispute ever since its discovery; some critics holding it to be the oldest example of Christian literature that we possess outside the New Testament, but others being unwilling to place it earlier than the middle of the second century.

* *H.E.* iii, 25 (Penguin edition, p. 134).　　　　† *Strom.* i, 20, 100.
‡ *Festal Letter* 39.

225

There is general agreement today that the book is in fact a composite affair, in which materials of an early date have been used by the compiler and touched up with additions and alterations of his own. The first portion (chapters 1 to 6), the Two Ways, has every appearance of being an ancient catechism of the pre-Christian era, over which our author has thrown just sufficient Christian colouring to make it usable for the instruction of candidates for baptism. In the second part (chapters 7 to 16) he has apparently laid hands on an old manual of Church regulations, made a few changes in it here and there, and added a final eschatological chapter of his own composition. To us it is the preservation of these old regulations that gives the *Didache* its unique interest and importance, for they reflect the life of a primitive Christian community somewhere in Syria (or possibly in Egypt) towards the close of the first century, at an epoch when travelling missioners were still the chief officers of the Church and bishops had not yet become distinguished from presbyters. In other words, they are the only piece of direct contemporary evidence that we have for the conditions of Church life during the obscure period which lies between the New Testament and the more fully developed organization of the second century. At what later date, however, the unknown Didachist put together the treatise in which he has embedded them, we have no means of discovering, though this is unlikely to have been later than A.D. 150.

The Didache

THE WAY OF LIFE

1. There are two Ways: a Way of Life and a Way of Death, and the difference between these two Ways is great.

The Way of Life is this: *Thou shalt love first the Lord thy Creator, and secondly thy neighbour as thyself; and thou shalt do nothing to any man that thou wouldst not wish to be done to thyself.*

What you may learn from those words is to bless them that curse you, to pray for your enemies, and to fast for your persecutors. For where is the merit in loving only those who return your love? Even the heathens do as much as that. But if you love those who hate you, you will have nobody to be your enemy.

Beware of the carnal appetites of the body. If someone strikes you on the right cheek, turn the other one to him as well, and perfection will be yours. Should anyone compel you to go a mile, go another one with him. If someone takes away your coat, let him have your shirt too. If someone seizes anything belonging to you, do not ask for it back again (you could not get it, anyway).[1] Give to everyone that asks, without looking for any repayment, for it is the Father's pleasure that we should share His gracious bounty with all men. A giver who gives freely, as the commandment directs, is blessed; no fault can be found with him. But woe to the taker; for though he cannot be blamed for taking if he was in need, yet if he was not, an account will be required of him as to why he took it, and for what purpose, and he will be taken into custody and examined about his action, and he will not get out until he has paid the last penny. The old saying is in point here: 'Let your alms grow damp with sweat in your hand, until you know who it is you are giving them to.'

2. The second commandment in the Teaching means: Commit no murder, adultery, sodomy, fornication, or theft. Practise no magic, sorcery, abortion, or infanticide. See that you do not covet anything your neighbour possesses, and never be guilty of perjury, false witness, slander, or malice. Do not equivocate in thought or speech, for a double tongue is a deadly snare; the words you speak should not be false or empty phrases, but fraught with purposeful action. You are not to be avaricious or extortionate, and you must resist any temptation to hypocrisy, spitefulness, or superiority. You are to have no malicious designs on a neighbour. You are to cherish no feelings of hatred for anybody; some you are to reprove, some to pray for, and some again to love more than your own life.

3. Keep away from every bad man, my son, and from all his kind. Never give way to anger, for anger leads to homicide. Likewise refrain from fanaticism, quarrelling, and hot-temperedness, for these too can breed homicide.

Beware of lust, my son, for lust leads to fornication. Likewise refrain from unclean talk and the roving eye, for these too can breed adultery.

Do not be always looking for omens, my son, for this leads to idolatry. Likewise have nothing to do with witchcraft, astrology, or magic; do not even consent to be a witness of such practices, for they too can all breed idolatry.

Tell no lies, my son, for lying leads to theft. Likewise do not be over-anxious to be rich or to be admired, for these too can breed thievishness.

Do not be a grumbler, my son, for this leads to blasphemy. Likewise do not be too opinionated, and do not harbour thought of wickedness, for these too can breed blasphemy.

Learn to be meek, for the meek are to inherit the earth. School yourself to forbearance, compassion, guilelessness, calmness, and goodness; and never forget to respect the teaching you have had.

Do not parade your own merits, or allow yourself to behave presumptuously, and do not make a point of associating with persons of eminence, but choose the companionship of honest and humble folk.

Accept as good whatever experience comes your way, in the knowledge that nothing can happen without God.

4. By day and by night, my son, remember him who speaks the word of God to you. Give him the honour you would give the Lord; for wherever the Lord's attributes are the subject of discourse, there the Lord is present. Frequent the company of the saints daily, so as to be edified by their conversation. Never encourage dissensions, but try to make peace between those who are at variance. Judge with justice, reprove without fear or favour, and never be in two minds about your decisions.

Do not be like those who reach out to take, but draw back when the time comes for giving. If the labour of your hands has been productive, make an offering as a ransom for your sins. Give without hesitating and without grumbling, and you will see Whose generosity will requite you. Never turn away the needy; share all your possessions with your brother, and do not claim that anything is your own. If you and he are joint participators in things immortal, how much more so in things that are mortal?

You are not to withhold your hand from your son or daughter, but to bring them up in the fear of God from their childhood.

Never speak sharply when giving orders to male or female domestics whose trust is in the same God as yours; otherwise they may cease to fear Him who is over you both. He has not come to call men according to their rank, but those who have been already prepared by the Spirit. And you, servants, obey your masters with respectfulness and fear, as the representatives of God. See that you do not neglect the commandments of the Lord, but keep them just as you received them, without any additions or subtractions of your own.

In church, make confession of your faults, and do not come to your prayers with a bad conscience.

That is the Way of Life.

THE WAY OF DEATH

5. The Way of Death is this. To begin with, it is evil, and in every way fraught with damnation. In it are murders, adulteries, lusts, fornications, thefts, idolatries, witchcraft, sorceries, robberies, perjuries, hypocrisies, duplicities, deceit, pride, malice, self-will, avarice, foul language, jealousy, insolence, arrogance, and boastfulness. Here are those who persecute good men, hold truth in abhorrence, and love falsehood; who do not know of the rewards of righteousness, nor adhere to what is good, nor to just judgement; who lie awake planning wickedness rather than well-doing. Gentleness and patience are beyond their conception; they care for nothing good or useful, and are bent only on their own advantage, without pity for the poor or feeling for the distressed. Knowledge of their Creator is not in them; they make away with their infants and deface God's image; they turn away the needy and oppress the afflicted; they aid and abet the rich but arbitrarily condemn the poor; they are utterly and altogether sunk in iniquity.

CONCLUSION

6. Take care that nobody tempts you away from the path of this Teaching, for such a man's tuition can have nothing to do with God. If you can shoulder the Lord's yoke in its entirety, then you will be perfect; but if that is too much for you, do as much as you can.

As regards diet, keep the rules so far as you are able; only be careful to refuse anything that has been offered to an idol, for that is the worship of dead gods.

PART 2. A CHURCH MANUAL

OF BAPTISM

7. The procedure for baptizing is as follows. After rehearsing all the preliminaries, immerse in running water 'In the Name of

the Father, and of the Son, and of the Holy Ghost'. If no running water is available, immerse in ordinary water. This should be cold if possible; otherwise warm. If neither is practicable, then sprinkle water three times on the head 'In the Name of the Father, and of the Son, and of the Holy Ghost'. Both baptizer and baptized ought to fast before the baptism, as well as any others who can do so; but the candidate himself should be told to keep a fast for a day or two beforehand.

OF FAST-DAYS AND PRAYER

8. Do not keep the same fast-days as the hypocrites.[2] Mondays and Thursdays are their days for fasting, so yours should be Wednesdays and Fridays.

Your prayers, too, should be different from theirs. Pray as the Lord enjoined in His Gospel, thus: Our Father, who art in heaven, Hallowed be thy Name, Thy kingdom come, Thy will be done, As in heaven, so on earth; Give us this day our daily bread, And forgive us our debt as we forgive our debtors, And lead us not into temptation, But deliver us from the Evil One, For thine is the power and the glory for ever and ever.

Say this prayer three times every day.

OF THE EUCHARIST[3]

9. At the Eucharist, offer the eucharistic prayer in this way. Begin with the chalice: 'We give thanks to thee, our Father, for the holy Vine[4] of thy servant David, which thou hast made known to us through thy servant Jesus.'

'Glory be to thee, world without end.'

Then over the particles of bread: 'We give thanks to thee, our Father; for the life and knowledge thou hast made known to us[5] through thy servant Jesus.'

'Glory be to thee, world without end.'

'As this broken bread, once dispersed over the hills, was brought together and became one loaf, so may thy Church be brought together from the ends of the earth into thy kingdom.'

'Thine is the glory and the power, through Jesus Christ, for ever and ever.'

No one is to eat or drink of your Eucharist but those who have been baptized in the Name of the Lord; for the Lord's own saying applies here, 'Give not that which is holy unto dogs.'

10. When all have partaken sufficiently, give thanks in these words:

'Thanks be to thee, holy Father, for thy sacred Name which thou hast caused to dwell in our hearts, and for the knowledge and faith and everlasting life which thou hast revealed to us through thy servant Jesus.'

'Glory be to thee for ever and ever.'

'Thou, O Almighty Lord, hast created all things for thine own Name's sake; to all men thou hast given meat and drink to enjoy, that they may give thanks to thee, but to us thou hast graciously given spiritual meat and drink, together with life eternal, through thy Servant. Especially, and above all, do we give thanks to thee for the mightiness of thy power.'

'Glory be to thee for ever and ever.'

'Be mindful of thy Church, O Lord; deliver it from all evil, perfect it in thy love, sanctify it, and gather it from the four winds into the kingdom which thou hast prepared for it.'

'Thine is the power and the glory for ever and ever.'

'Let His Grace draw near,[6] and let this present world pass away.'

'Hosanna to the God of David.'

'Whosoever is holy, let him approach. Whoso is not, let him repent.'

'O Lord, come quickly. Amen.'

(Charismatists, however, should be free to give thanks as they please.)

OF MISSIONERS AND CHARISMATISTS[7]

11. If anyone comes and instructs you on the foregoing lines, make him welcome. But should the instructor himself then turn round and introduce teaching of a different and subversive

nature, pay no attention to him. If it aims at promoting righteousness and knowledge of the Lord, though, welcome him as you would the Lord.

As regards missioners and charismatists, according to the Gospel directions this is how you are to act. Every missioner who comes to you should be welcomed as the Lord, but he is not to stay more than a day, or two days if it is really necessary. If he stays for three days, he is no genuine missioner. And a missioner at his departure should accept nothing but as much provisions as will last him to his next night's lodging. If he asks for money, he is not a genuine missioner.

While a charismatist is uttering words in a trance, you are on no account to subject him to any tests or verifications; *every sin shall be forgiven, but this sin shall not be forgiven.** [8] Nevertheless, not all who speak in trances are charismatists, unless they also exhibit the manners and conduct of the Lord. It is by their behaviour that you can tell the impostor from the true. Thus, if a charismatist should happen to call out for something to eat while he is in his trance, he will not actually eat of it; if he does, he is a fraud. Also, even supposing a charismatist is sound enough in his teaching, yet if his deeds do not correspond with his words he is an impostor. Or again, a charismatist, thoroughly accredited and genuine, may set forth some mystery of the Church by his actions, and yet fail to teach others to copy his example. In that case, you are not to judge the man yourselves; his judgement lies with God. The prophets of old used to do things of a similar kind.

If any charismatist, speaking in a trance, says, 'Give me money (or anything else)', do not listen to him. On the other hand, if he bids you give it to someone else who is in need, nobody should criticize him.

12. Everyone who comes 'in the Name of the Lord' is to be made welcome, though later on you must test him and find out about him. You will be able to distinguish the true from the false. If the newcomer is only passing through, give him all the help you can – though he is not to stay more than a couple of

* *Matthew* xii, 31.

days with you, or three if it is unavoidable. But if he wants to settle down among you, and is a skilled worker, let him find employment and earn his bread. If he knows no trade, use your discretion to make sure that he does not live in idleness simply on the strength of being a Christian. Unless he agrees to this, he is only trying to exploit Christ. You must be on your guard against men of that sort.

13. A genuine charismatist, however, who wishes to make his home with you has a right to a livelihood. (Similarly, a genuine teacher is as much entitled to his keep as a manual labourer.) You are therefore to take the first products of your winepress, your threshing-floor, your oxen and your sheep, and give them as firstfruits to the charismatists, for nowadays it is they who are your 'High Priests'. If there is no charismatist among you, give them to the poor. And when you bake a batch of loaves, take the first of them and give it away, as the commandment directs. Similarly when you broach a jar of wine or oil, take the first portion to give to the charismatists. So, too, with your money, and your clothing, and all your possessions; take a tithe of them in whatever way you think best, and make a gift of it, as the commandment bids you.

OF SUNDAY WORSHIP

14. Assemble on the Lord's Day, and break bread and offer the Eucharist; but first make confession of your faults, so that your sacrifice may be a pure one. Anyone who has a difference with his fellow is not to take part with you until they have been reconciled, so as to avoid any profanation of your sacrifice. For this is the offering of which the Lord has said, *Everywhere and always bring me a sacrifice that is undefiled, for I am a great king, says the Lord, and my name is the wonder of nations.*[*]

OF LOCAL OFFICIALS

15. You must choose for yourselves overseers and assistants[9] who are worthy of the Lord: men who are humble and not

[*] *Malachi* i, 11, 14.

eager for money, but sincere and approved; for they are carrying out the ministry of the charismatists and teachers for you. Do not esteem them lightly, for they take an honourable rank among you along with the charismatists and catechists.

Reprove one another, but peaceably and not in hot blood, as you are told in the Gospel. But have no converse with anyone who has done his neighbour an injury; let that man not hear a single word from you until he repents.

In your prayers, your almsgiving, and everything you do, be guided by what you read in the Gospel of our Lord.

ESCHATOLOGY

16. Be watchful over your life; never let your lamps go out or your loins be ungirt, but keep yourselves always in readiness, for you can never be sure of the hour when our Lord may be coming. Come often together for spiritual improvement; because all the past years of your faith will be no good to you at the end, unless you have made yourselves perfect. In the last days of the world false prophets and deceivers will abound, sheep will be perverted and turn into wolves, and love will change to hate, for with the growth of lawlessness men will begin to hate their fellows and persecute them and betray them. Then the Deceiver of the World will show himself, pretending to be a Son of God and doing signs and wonders, and the earth will be delivered into his hands, and he will work such wickedness as there has never been since the beginning. After that, all humankind will come up for their fiery trial; multitudes of them will stumble and perish, but such as remain steadfast in the faith will be saved by the Curse.[10] And then the signs of the truth will appear: first the sign of the opening heavens, next the sign of the trumpet's voice, and thirdly the rising of the dead – not of all the dead, but, as it says, *the Lord will come, and with him all his holy ones.** And then the whole world will see the Lord as He comes riding on the clouds of heaven.

* *Zechariah* xiv, 5.

NOTES

1. A sidelight on the helplessness of the poor Christian community in a pagan society.

2. i.e. the Jews.

3. The repeated doxologies in this and the next chapter suggest that they are responses to be made by the congregation, and I have therefore printed them accordingly.

4. This may be either a term for Christ (cf. *John* xv, 1), or for the eucharistic Blood, or perhaps for the Church of God (*Ps.* lxxx).

5. i.e. the eternal life (*John* iii, 15) and the knowledge of God (*II Corinthians* iv, 6) which are Christ's gifts to men.

6. 'Grace' is a synonym for Christ.

7. Missioners and Charismatists. I have ventured to substitute these titles for the 'apostles' and 'prophets' of the Greek text, which might mislead some readers. It must be remembered that the organization of the primitive Church was not the system with which we are familiar today. During the first period of its life the Church was very directly under the rule and guidance of the Holy Ghost. This resulted in the emergence of three classes of officials, whose names are given us by St Paul: 'God', he says, 'hath set in the church first apostles, second-arily prophets, thirdly teachers'.* All these were men who had been directly called to their office by the Holy Ghost; they were not appointed by any local congregation, nor was their ministry confined to any local church. The 'apostles' were travelling missionaries or evangelists, who went about founding new churches and visiting and edifying others; the 'prophets' were men with the gift of revealing spiritual truths while in trances or ecstasies; the 'teachers' were en-dowed with special powers of instruction and exposition. To supple-ment this itinerant ministry, there were resident officers in each local church; who, however, were more concerned with administration and discipline than with teaching and preaching. These were the 'bishops' or 'presbyters' (until the second century either name was used in-differently to denote the one functionary) and their helpers the 'deacons'. When in due course the inspired race of apostles, prophets and teachers died out, this local ministry succeeded to the leadership, developing presently out of a twofold into a threefold form, with a single bishop ruling the church, a council of presbyters as his assessors, and the deacons to see to the relief of the poor and needy.

* *I Corinthians* xii, 28.

8. Because to doubt the authenticity of the charismatist's inspiration is a blasphemy against the Holy Ghost Who inspires him.

9. Overseers and assistants. The Greek words are *episcopoi* and *diaconoi*, whence the English 'bishops' and 'deacons'.

10. The meaning is obscure. Perhaps it may allude to Christ, who was 'made a curse for us' (*Galatians* iii, 13).

A NOTE ON THE TYPE

The text of this book is set in Granjon which was designed for Linotype under the supervision of George W. Jones about 1928. Granjon is the closest contemporary reproduction of the types of Claude Garamond (1480-1561). The typeface called Garamond in use today is based on the types cut by Jean Jannon in Sedan in 1615.

270.1
Early
    Early Christian writings